T0197349

# FINDING TRUTH

# FINDING TRUTH

## The Guide for Police Investigators, Interrogators, & Everyday Interviewers

(BECOME A LIE-DETECTOR USING
BIBLICAL STRATEGY)

## JJ. WILLSON

### HOUSTON HOMICIDE SERGEANT
### (RETIRED)

authorHOUSE®

*AuthorHouse™*
*1663 Liberty Drive*
*Bloomington, IN 47403*
*www.authorhouse.com*
*Phone: 1 (800) 839-8640*

*NKJV*
*Scripture quotations marked NKJV are taken from the New King James Version. Copyright © 1982 by Thomas Nelson, Inc. Used by permission. All rights reserved.*

*\*Scripture taken from Todays English Version (TEV): Second Edition, Copyright 1992 Old Testament: American Bible Society 1976, 1992 New Testament: American Bible Society 1966, 1971, 1976, 1992.*

*\*Scripture quotations marked (HCSB) have been taken from the Holman Christian Standard Bible. Copyright 1999, 2000, 2002, 2003, 2009 by Holman Bible Publishers. Used by permission. Holman Christian Standard Bible, Holman CSB, and HCSB are federally registered trademarks of Holman Bible Publishers.*

*Published by AuthorHouse 3/23/2015*

*ISBN: 978-1-4969-7417-4 (sc)*
*ISBN: 978-1-4969-7415-0 (e)*

*Library of Congress Control Number: 2015904368*

*Print information available on the last page.*

*Any people depicted in stock imagery provided by Thinkstock are models, and such images are being used for illustrative purposes only. Certain stock imagery © Thinkstock.*

*This book is printed on acid-free paper.*

# TABLE OF CONTENTS

# SPECIAL THANKS

This book is dedicated to all law enforcement officers (past and present) that have stood strong on the "thin blue line" of law and justice. God tells us in Proverbs 27:17 that, "As iron sharpens iron, one man will sharpen another." I am hopeful that this book will assist and sharpen the skills of law enforcement officers everywhere as they study the content and apply it to their criminal cases.

A special thanks to every church that ever helped me in FINDING TRUTH through Gods word and sustaining me in his everlasting love. From the Caribbean Virgin Islands to the Northern Rocky Mountains of Montana, I sincerely appreciate your passion and welcoming words.

I will never forget the little white wood-framed country church in Carlos, Texas. Thank you for allowing me to speak into your lives with my prayers, pondering, and wondering of God's mysterious ways.

# INTRODUCTION

*(Sorting through trash to find the truth)*

———◦((◦))◦———

Every day, in millions of places around the world, millions of people are gathering information through verbal exchange communication. It is the old fashioned face-to-face human contact that no computer email or cell phone could ever replace. Social network sites allow for rapid fire responses and texts from cell phones are convenient. However, a "My-Face or Insta-Chat" account will never out-perform the precision of truth found in face-to-face communication. In law enforcement, good communication is paramount in performing our duties. Every traffic accident, every domestic disturbance, and every crime scene will require the officer to communicate and come to a conclusion. From the young rookie street cop to the salty, old, seasoned detective, all law enforcement personnel must gather information through the same face-to-face interview process. The goal is simple and straight forward, to separate truth from trash and sort out fact from fiction.

Some people like to quote the Bible and say "The truth will set you free." The scripture actually reads in John 8:32

(HCSB),"You will know the truth, and the truth will set you free." It is the truth that we know in law enforcement that sets us free to solve the case, stop the crime, and prevent evil from prospering. Truth will not set you free unless it is known. If we would have known the truth about September 11, 2001, on September 10, 2001, then we would have been set free from a terrorist attack in New York City and no one would have been killed.

As a retired Houston Homicide Detective, I have attended many classes, courses, and training seminars on the art of interviewing and interrogating people. In my 27 year cop career, I have interviewed thousands of people with good, bad, and ugly results. Before I learned the strategy, I often muddled my way through it. However, all this training and experience does not compare to following God's strategy in the Holy Bible. There is no greater truth seeker than God's word and no greater teacher than God's patterns and principles taught in the Bible. God rarely repeats himself in the Bible, but when he does, we need to pay close attention. One such place where God repeats himself is the scripture of Genesis 1:27 (HCSB) which says, "So God created man in his own image. He created him in the image of God. He created them male and female." The Creator put his own character inside of his own creation and God gave us spirit through the Holy Spirit. Although we don't always act Godly, we have the same God-given ability to create, reason, and construct. We didn't evolve from the beginning of time; we were equipped from the beginning of time. God has the secret recipe to make mankind and the only ingredient is himself. As we study nature, we see a similar pattern with insects using themselves in production. Honey bees use themselves and have the only secret recipe to make honey. No living species has ever reproduced honey except the honey bee. Anything else is cheap imitation made with corn syrup, but not the original creation.

If all people have the image of God in them, then inside of every person is the truth that wants to be known and announced. No matter how evil or awful that we believe a person is, there is truth in them that wants to be set free. Somewhere deep inside the heart of every psychopath and sociopath is the truth fighting to get out. This is why even seasoned career criminals will confess when it does not benefit them. Truth must flow free and come out. If they do not tell the police, they will tell a priest, a cell mate, a girlfriend, or anyone who will listen. If we can remember this one nugget of knowledge as police officers conducting the interview, we will be successful in getting the confession. We must attempt to peel away the layers of humanity and get to the image of God, which is truth. We know that God is truth because he says so in John 14:6 (HCSB); "Jesus said, I am the way, the TRUTH, and the life. No one comes to the father except through me." Truth does not belong in the darkness but wants to be shouted from the roof tops. Everyone in law enforcement should understand and utilize this concept if the interviewing process is going to be successful. Sometimes as we interview people, we must get past years of abuse, anger, chaos, and confusion to tap into the truth. It is similar to cracking the hard shell of a coconut. The outer layers of the coconut must be cracked and removed so the sweet coconut milk and meat will be revealed. The truth will flow free once the hard outer layer is cracked open. This is why confessions and admissions sometimes take hours, days, or even years. The hard shell of humanity builds up around the sweet truth.

Another fact that everyone involved in law enforcement needs to know is that God is on your side and considers you one of his children. The Bible clearly tells police officers in Matthew 5:9 (HCSB), "The peacemakers are blessed, for they will be called sons of God." If we are peace officers, then we are also peace makers. If we are sons of God, then we are not unclaimed orphans or outcasts. Our badge means that we belong, and our God says that we are strong. There will always be self-serving community activists organizing the so called "peaceful protests" that openly promote and declare our deaths. However, when the smoke clears, we will prevail and be protected because God is on our side.

# FLESH WILL NEVER CONFESS

*(Why people do what they don't want to do)*

# CHAPTER 1

Some may be reading this book and say, "I thought this was a book about police interviews; I didn't know we were going to church." Please let me first explain the order of things. The scientists and engineers of NASA had to fully understand the invisible laws of gravity before they designed the first visible plan for a rocket to reach space. I am starting with that which is invisible, so you can clearly understand that which is visible and make it work.

Most people have heard of the "Holy Trinity" of God. He is God the Father, God the Son, and God the Holy Spirit. Trinity means "three in unity" so God is all three, but he is still one God. We as people are created in his image, so we are designed in the same way. We were created as a human trinity, three-in-one just like God. We are made up of a body, a spirit, and a soul. Our body (flesh) always has a desire to satisfy itself and serve its own agenda. It wants to rest, it wants to eat, it wants to drink, and it wants to have sex. None of these things are bad unless we let our body (flesh) control our lives and pursue the fleshly desires with excess. This is why in our society today we see slothful sleepers, binge eaters, drug abusers, alcoholics, and sex maniacs. Some people abuse these things and go beyond moderation.

The second part of a human being is our spirit. God instilled inside every person a spirit that has a passion for the purpose of God. Our spirit is always trying to connect with the Holy Spirit. This is why people have a conscience to know the difference between good and evil. Without anyone ever teaching a person to do so, the spirit will naturally pursue that which is good and that which is from God. Even an atheist can appreciate the beauty of a tree or a sunset; even though they deny God, their true passion is for the Creator of the tree and the sunset. Life is more than a heartbeat and a brain wave; it is the passion to pursue something good. The Declaration of Independence describes it best as "Life, liberty, and the pursuit of happiness." The reason that people choose to do bad things is that they are not led by a spirit that pursues God but are led by their fleshly desires. The Bible says in Galatians 5:16 (HCSB), "Walk by the spirit, and you will not carry out the desire of the flesh."

The last part of the human being is our soul, which is made up of the mind, will, and emotion. We think, feel, and draw our opinions from our soul. Inside of the human body is a daily and constant tug-of-war struggle for the soul of a human being. The flesh wants to satisfy itself so pulls on the soul to follow it. The spirit wants to pursue good and Godly things, so it pulls on the soul to follow it as well. The soul is caught in the middle so it can be pulled in either direction with different agendas. King David understood this concept thousands of years ago as he spoke out in the scriptures at Psalm 103:1 (NKJV), "Bless the Lord, O my soul, and all that is within me. Bless His Holy Name." David was literally telling his soul to submit and draw close to God.

To be successful at interviews and interrogations in seeking the truth, every law enforcement officer must pull on the soul (mind, will, and emotion) of a person. It's not hard once you use God given principles found in the Holy Bible. God revealed how to detect deception and how to seek the truth in an interview. If we follow God's strategy, we will pick up signals, much like a lie detector, when a suspect is being deceptive and truth is being hidden and held back.

As you interview a person, understand that flesh will never confess because it does not benefit the flesh to confess. In other words, a body does not want to be locked up in a steel jail cell or eat cold prison food. The body (fleshly desires) will always attempt to pull the soul away from the truth of a confession. Jesus plainly says in Mark 14:38 (HCSB), "The spirit is willing, but the flesh is weak." Confession comes from the soul (mind, will, and emotion) of a person which was influenced by the spirit. We, as the interviewer, are simply a tour guide to direct and influence people to move their soul from faulty thinking to truthful thinking.

# HOW ARE YA IN HAWAII?

*(How to manage & maintain the interview)*

## CHAPTER 2

———◆◉◆———

All newly arriving Houston Homicide Detectives are expected to go through a series of classes to help with investigation and interrogation skills. One memorable class taught newly assigned investigators how to work in the interview room with the greatest chance of success. Houston has up-to-date interview rooms where the room has been soundproofed, video-equipped, and wired for sound. The police interview room is the best place to record a verbal conversation in private without outside influence. Some detectives preferred using written confessions in their cases, but written documents have lost some credibility in recent years in the courtroom. Even a half-hearted defense attorney will dispute the written confession by their client and say that it was created through water boarding or some other instrument of torture. If a suspect insist on writing his confession out, video the event of the actual document as the suspect reads it and signs it. Many suspects have had buyer's remorse; so claimed that they were forced to sign their name to a blank sheet of paper, and the confession was printed on the paper after they left the police station.

I learned years ago from top-notch Homicide Detectives that the video interview room is the investigators stage and the jury can be the suspense-filled audience. This boring and boxy room is where the investigator creates his finest masterpieces in police work. This is the place where the suspect is most likely to cave-in and confess to his crime because he is alone with his soul and the soul searcher, which is you. The event of the private video interview usually has the greatest shot at success. However, all distractions and attractions must be removed from the room. The ideal interview room must have no windows or view of the outside world. The ideal interview room must have no pictures, photos, decorations, or any object that would allow someone to take a virtual tour away from the interview. The suspect can avoid the truth spoken in the interview if he is allowed to drift away and day dream as he looks at your vacation photos from Hawaii. Keep all walls, desks, and floors clear of any object that would allow a mind trip to Hawaii, traveling far away from the confession.

The interview and interrogation of a person suspected of a crime is a psychological mind game. You want to know what he knows, and he wants to know what you know, so the game plays on. Set the stage to win the game and make every advantage count. Make sure the furniture in the interview room is prearranged so the suspect cannot place himself behind any table, desk, or chair. No barriers or restrictions should be allowed between the investigator and the suspect because you will be turning up the tension and crowding in closer to him as the interview is concluded. Before he becomes vulnerable and opens up to you emotionally, you will need him to be vulnerable and open up physically. Make sure the suspect's chair has no rollers and sits flatly on four legs, preferably with arm rests so he can't lean away from you to escape. Your chair should have rollers as you will be moving closer to him as the interview progresses.

Before you enter the interview room, make sure that the suspect has already waited in there at least 10 minutes, so he will be waiting on you and not you waiting on him. As you enter the interview room, bring a case file with the suspects name on it, even if you have nothing on the case yet. The suspect needs to have the perception that a team of detectives is working the case and very close to uncovering the truth, even if you're the lone ranger investigator. I often brought a thick case file with fake fingerprint samples intentionally sticking out to create an illusion that fingerprints were recovered from the crime scene. As you walk in the room, introduce yourself without using your rank or a title because you need to be seen as a person he can trust and not a police officer that will take his freedom away. Leave your duty weapon and handcuffs out of the interview room as there is a fine balancing act of having authority without showing authority. Ask him to state his name and make sure that he is seated in the predetermined chair as the video will be recording at this point. Do not offer a handshake as you greet him unless he offers first. Even though you already know his formal name, ask him what he would like to be called so you can gain his trust and build rapport during questioning. Believe it or not, a guy named Harold felt more at ease being called by his biker gang name of "Cock Skull." The school principal, parole officer, and all authority figures called him by his formal name. However, all his friends knew him as "Cock Skull" so we must become a friend and use the desired name. If you are interviewing someone of a certain profession, avoid using the title of their occupation. Get on a "first name" basis with them, but do not allow their authority to override you in the interview room. For example, always avoid: Dr. Dogooder, Sgt. Selfish, or Pastor Pridefill.

Offer the suspect the use of restroom facilities, water, coffee, and even food before the interview starts. This serves two purposes as people begin to trust those that feed them, and the jury will see that you didn't use starvation or dehydration to obtain a confession. Remember, this is not a death row execution, so there will be no "last meal" requests. No steak or lobster dinners offered, just have somebody make a quick food run to the local "Mack in the Box." I have never met a vegetarian serial killer, so I have eaten many cheeseburgers with suspects as we talked about a gruesome killing. Keep the conversation light at first and get the suspect to answer "Yes" to obvious questions, "Did you get enough to eat?" or "Wasn't that some good coffee?" This is a classic car salesman approach that if someone says "Yes" enough times in conversation, then saying "No" will become harder in confrontation when the deal is offered.

The biggest attention to detail for a police investigator is to honor the U.S. Constitution, as cases have been lost by ignoring it. As police officers, we are held to a higher standard and under a constant microscope. We must promote the preservation of Fifth Amendment rights of the accused regarding self-incrimination. Every police cadet in every academy has studied the case of Miranda vs Arizona (1966). We know how to "mirandize" the accused in police custody being questioned about the crime. Each U.S. State has their own slightly modified version of the Fifth Amendment Miranda Warning. However, there are certain words that must be presented to those in police custody being questioned. I always read it verbatim from the card to get it exactly right, and always ask the accused if he understands after each question is presented. For example:

"You have the right to remain silent and not say anything at all; do you understand?"

"If you give up that right, it can be used against you in a court of law; do you understand?"

"You have a right to have an attorney present; do you understand?"

"If you can't afford an attorney then one will be provided; do you understand?"

"Can we talk about some issues to clear this matter up?"

After making small talk about coffee and food and then reading the required Miranda Warning to the suspect, you will have gotten him to answer "Yes" to about six to eight questions. When you ask the question of "Can we talk?" he has already said "Yes" to everything else asked of him. He will now be more likely to be in agreement and give a final "Yes" before the interview starts. Sometimes a suspect will ask questions about incriminating himself, and this is good thing because it shows that he is trusting you enough to inquire about his future. For example, I have had suspects ask the following:

Q: "Do you think I need an attorney?"

A: "I'm only looking for the truth, we can talk if you're telling the truth."

*Another example:

Q: "Should I remain silent?"

A: "If you were asking me questions that needed to be cleared up, wouldn't you want me to talk and explain the truth to you?"

*Another example:

Q: "Can we work out a deal if I tell you what happened?"

A: "If you deserve a break in the case, then the defense attorney and the district attorney might be able to work something out."

Notice how I didn't really answer any of the three questions, but simply minimized my statements to bring maximum impact. If the suspect indicates "No" and requests an attorney, federal law requires that law enforcement must wait 14 days before attempting another interview. This law was implemented in a 2010 U.S. Supreme Court Case, so I have often used it to my advantage. I have had attorney's call me very angry and advise me not to speak with their client any more about a certain case. However, the accused must make their own choices and refuse the questions asked of them. No attorney can invoke the client's rights for him if the client is freely speaking. There is no statute of limitations on murder, so I have interrogated some suspects years after they have already "lawyered up." It is amazing how time can draw out the truth and get the coconut milk to flow. Remember, make no promises or back-room deals that you do not have the authority to keep. As the investigator, you are the tour guide taking the suspect to the destination of a confession, not the travel agent promising to get him to Hawaii.

# THROWING THE VELVET COVERED BRICK

*(Strategy for gaining trust & getting truth)*

# CHAPTER 3

———◦◦◦◦———

To get a confession as a police officer means that you are getting someone to admit to a wrongful act or have knowledge of a wrongful act and be willing to go public with it. Court documents are public records, so once the case is resolved then all the world has access to it. When someone confesses their sin to a priest or psychologist, then there is an expectation of privacy. The one confessing and being counseled can stay private and fly below the radar, so no public opinion will form against them. Police officers live by a different code, so no confession stays private and no evidence stays hidden.

To get someone to talk about their crime and reveal their wrongful behavior to the world requires empathy and sympathy from the interviewer. In other words, people want to know that you understand them and will not condemn them. I refer to this method of getting confessions as

"Throwing the velvet-covered brick." What I have to offer as a police investigator must have the appearance of being soft and smooth, even though there is brutal truth underneath it that will hit them hard. It is similar to a surgery being performed where the nurse comforts you before the doctor cuts you. I know as a police officer that the confession of the suspect will likely lead to the conviction of the suspect, but truth must come out and trash will be thrown out.

In the Bible at John Chapter 8, several self-righteous priests drag a woman that was caught in the act of adultery to appear before Jesus. They apparently caught her in a sexual act, so there was physical evidence as well as circumstantial evidence against her. The case was strong, and they had already accused her and abused her by dragging her into public view. We see no signs of empathy or sympathy from the priests as they tell Jesus in verse 5 (TEV), "In our law, Moses commanded that such a woman must be stoned to death. Now, what do you say?" At this point, the woman felt embarrassed and condemned and had not said a word to anyone, much less given a confession. Jesus sidesteps their accusations and quickly connects with the woman as he leans down near the dirt where she lay. He gets on the same level with her in the dirt, because she was obviously feeling like dirt. Jesus said in verse 7 (TEV), "Whichever one of you has committed no sin may throw the first stone at her." In other words, "It is true that she has sinned, but so have all of you who accuse her and drag her here." Jesus was showing empathy and sympathy to the woman to let her know that she was not alone because the entire crowd had sin issues.

Jesus minimized the crime in order to maximize the change in her life. The Bible says that the crowd dropped their rocks (velvet less bricks) and walked away one by one leaving Jesus alone with the woman. Notice, how Jesus does not start the interview process until all the spectators have left and there are no distractions. We, as police interviewers, need to learn from this example. A one-on-one interview will always produce the most success. Jesus is teaching us textbook interview techniques using empathy, sympathy, and getting on the same level with people. He starts the interview with a question to ask her where all her accusers went, indicating that he was not one of the accusers. For the very first time in the story, we hear the woman speak as she obviously trusted Jesus enough to talk with him. As Jesus said in verse 10 (TEV), "Is there anyone left to condemn you?" The woman answers, "No one, Lord." (NKJV). Her answer indicates that she knows Jesus truly understands and comprehends her and will not condemn her. She places her trust in him, so also shares her truth with him. Jesus is now able to speak bluntly to the woman, and has impacted her because he has made contact with her. He tells her, "Go, but do not sin again." There is no denial or deception from the woman, there is only relief that the truth is known and it sets her free.

As you interview a subject and prepare to throw the velvet-covered brick, there are some sensitive words that you should avoid:

Avoid saying "confess"; use "tell the truth."

Avoid saying "interrogate" or "interview"; use "talk to me."

Avoid saying "murder" or "assault"; use "shoot," "stab," or "hurt."

Avoid saying "kidnap" or "carjack"; use "take" or "control."

Avoid saying "jury" or "trial"; use "people" or "public."

Avoid saying "arrest" or "prison"; use "lose your freedom."

Avoid saying "testify" or "under oath"; use "tell the story."

Avoid saying "strangle" or "suffocate"; use "grab" or "hold."

Avoid saying "liar" or "you lied"; use "not given the whole truth."

Avoid saying "beat" or "torture"; use "hit" or "hurt."

Avoid saying "rape" or "sexual assault; use "having sex without consent."

By minimizing the crime and avoiding certain terms, you will keep communication flowing and keep the velvet wrapped around the brick. Whenever the subject mentions these words first, then it is acceptable as an investigator to use the same words in conversation. However, let the subject confess his wrongful actions; you are just the tour guide getting him to that destination.

The question of freedom is at the fore-front of the thought process during an interrogation. If handcuffs are on the suspect, then remove the handcuffs before you begin the interview. He is losing his freedom but doesn't need a reminder of it. If the suspect is in the back of a police car, climb in the back of the police car with him to conduct the pre-interview. Sometimes a back seat confession comes quickly, so keep your camcorder close by in case the pre-interview brings a clean conscience. If the suspect is in a police interview room, then you must enter the room as person of compassion and offer him a drink, food, and the use of restroom facilities before the interview starts. Remember that you are about to hit him with the proverbial velvet-covered brick, so bring the softness of velvet before hitting him with the hardness of the brick truth. You must get to his level and get in the dirt with him, just as Jesus did in John Chapter 8 to gain trust and get the communication going. No person will ever confess to someone that does not understand or care about their situation. Show that you care and show that you have compassion. You must obtain the confession of the crime in order to guarantee the conviction of the crime.

# THE TITANIC KEEPS SINKING

*(Making an impact with people)*

# CHAPTER 4

I often got teased and laughed at in the Homicide Division because I would tell crazy stories to suspects to get them to talk and speak the truth. Some detectives use different strategies, so they talk less and tolerate less. However, I used a style that worked consistently, and I saw no reason to change it. The way I approach an interview is the same way that I approach my own children. If my little boy is running with sharp scissors in his hand, I could certainly yell, "You knucklehead, don't run with that in your hand!" Sure, I have sent him a message, but I would rather have him learn a lesson from his experience. I tell him a story to paint a picture in his mind. I create a visual that my son can remember, so I tell him about one of my childhood mishaps or hurtful accidents so he can relate to it. In other words, I find a theme to a story that will get his attention and impact him.

The interview process works the same way in six-year-olds or serial killers. Find a theme and tell a story because you must make contact with a person's emotions if you are going to impact a person's emotions. Here is a good one liner to remember, "No contact means no impact." Most people have seen the movie <u>Titanic</u>, so I often used it as a theme for my interviews. Sometimes in homicide investigations, we have multiple suspects for one murder; one proven strategy is to get them to turn against each other. I once was interviewing a prostitute who was involved with other prostitutes in the murder of their date (client) for the night. As I spoke with the co-defendant prostitute suspected in the homicide, I informed her that we were going to catch all the parties involved and the case would be cleared soon. I was actually bluffing and the only thing that I was sure of was that I didn't commit the murder. I started with the Titanic themed story to grab her attention. I compared her murder case to the sinking of the Titanic to show the analogy. I began with the idea that her life was like a cruise ship. She was on board and being entertained by "wining and dining, blowing and going" without any real destination. However, a killing appeared out of nowhere like an iceberg in the night and the Titanic hit it hard. I continued by explaining that there are not enough life boats for everyone, so not everyone can be saved. The Titanic is going to slowly sink so she needed to get on a life boat quickly before she sank to the dark depths of the icy ocean. She would be given one opportunity to save herself and give the names of all the people that were involved in the killing. Based on the Titanic story line and painting a proverbial picture for the prostitute to see, she saw a life boat and jumped on. All four of the suspects' names were given, identified, and later arrested for Capital Murder. The proverbial Titanic has sunk multiple times during my many interviews.

Another successful interview that I conducted was with a cold-hearted boyfriend who had killed his girlfriend's three-year-old son. The unemployed boyfriend often provided daycare for the little boy while the mother worked and also attended college classes. The little boy suddenly started showing a lot of bruising on his body, but the boyfriend always explained it away with lame excuses. One night, the mother came home exhausted because of a full-time schedule of work and school so she went to sleep early. The boyfriend was left to take care of the little boy as he had been doing all day without a break. The boyfriend tried to get the little boy to lie down and go to sleep, but the child was fussy because he missed the attention and affection of his mother. The boyfriend became frustrated, not wanting the little boy to wake the mother, so he lost his temper and the child lost his life. After the murder, the boyfriend simply tucked the dead child back into his cute little race-car bed, and calmly walked out of the room to go sleep with the mother. I attended the autopsy of the three-year-old boy; the pathologist showed me signs of months of internal bruising and abuse. The doctor took out the liver of the child and showed me where it had been hit with such force that it was almost severed in half. I knew I had my work cut out for me because the boyfriend was already claiming that someone had broken into their apartment through the back door and killed the little boy while they slept. The door showed signs of forced entry, but the boyfriend showed signs of deception as well.

In the interview room, I hid my disgust of what the boyfriend had done to the child, because I knew I needed to connect with him emotionally. The velvet-covered brick had to be thrown and the hard truth was going to hurt. First, I had to gain his trust and get on his level. I knew I needed to pull his soul towards a confession for the truth to be revealed. I began with a story that the boyfriend could relate to and used a theme that he could easily understand. I explained to the boyfriend that I also have a little boy, and he has a small pony to ride. One day when I took my son out to the field, I told him he could ride the pony anywhere in the open pasture, but he had to keep the pony away from trees. I explained to my son that if he rode the pony under the trees, the pony would use the branches of the trees to sweep him off the saddle. At this point, I asked the boyfriend, "What do you think my son did with the pony?" The boyfriend smiled and asked "Did he ride under the trees and get knocked off?" I knew then that I had chosen the right story line because the boyfriend was accepting and relating to the story about my son. I asked the boyfriend, "Have you ever gotten frustrated with a child because you teach them to do right and they choose to do wrong?" The boyfriend kept smiling and acknowledged that he had gotten frustrated in the past with kids that don't listen. I had given the boyfriend his escape from the reality of the murder by minimizing the crime as I said to him, "We're adults and we know what's best for a child, but they don't listen so they get hurt." I continued by explaining that my son had bruises all over him after falling from the saddle, but he would not have been hurt if he had just obeyed. The boyfriend stayed glued to my story and I could see that he was emotionally connected and trusted me. At this point, I asked him, "Is that what happened to you? Did the child not obey so he got hurt?" The boyfriend lowered his head, said "Yes," and admitted that the child would not listen to him and would not stay in bed. The boyfriend admitted that he punched the child repeatedly in the stomach, in order to knock the air out of him with no detectable marks. He had simply wanted to silence the child but lost his temper in the process. The boyfriend confessed and told the whole sad story of the little boy's last minutes of life.

My story had impacted him to tell his story. In a connected, twisted way, he could relate his story of beating a child to death and compare it to my story of a child falling from a pony. I am convinced that without the emotional connection, no impact would have been made and no confession would have been given. Truth was sought after and the Capital Murder case was rock solid for conviction. Remember, no contact means no impact.

Jesus walked through hillsides and villages and met with people who lived in poverty or lived with plenty. He always bonded with people through stories they could emotionally relate to and feel a connection. Jesus told so many stories in the Bible that we now refer to them as "parables." In other words, Jesus used his parables to parallel peoples' lives, so they would accept and not reject the message. Jesus knew his audience and knew what it took to convict a heart and change a life. As Jesus walked the Earth, he never once failed to find the perfect theme that made the most impact with the people. No amount of Ivy League education or human behavior study could compare to the strategy of this carpenter named Jesus. He was the greatest communicator that the world has ever seen. Two thousand years later, we are still talking about this ordinary man with an extraordinary ability to get people to admit their sin and turn to him.

# I KNOW NOTHIIING...
# I SEE NOTHIIING

*(Getting the guilty to open up)*

# CHAPTER 5

———◦◉◦———

Years ago, a weekly television show about a guy named "Hogan" hit American viewers by storm. It was a goofy series about "Heroes" from the war era that made fun of the Nazis of World War II. The story line was based on captured soldiers inside the concentration camps, and how they plotted to survive and outsmart the enemy. It turned a very serious subject into comedy as the inmates secretly ran the asylum. One of the prison guards named Sgt. Schultz was an unforgettable character. Sgt. Schultz was big burly man that completely filled out his Nazi uniform, but left his helmet empty of any brains. Sgt. Schultz was a strong soldier but had a weakness for food. He would walk through the prisoner barracks daily to monitor them and try to uncover their escape plan. The prisoners knew his weakness, so they would often bribe him and buy his silence with cakes, cookies, and pies. After the bribe, Sgt. Schultz would always deliver his most memorable excuse and disclaimer. He would snap to attention and sound off with a resounding "I know nothiiing...I see nothiiing!" To this day, I often imitate Sgt. Schultz and keep my kids laughing at this ridiculous statement.

If you interview or interrogate people for any period of time, you will meet the proverbial Sgt. Schultz. These types of people have a hunger to be self-serving and will tell you nothing because it benefits you and not them. In their eyes, you are less important than their self-inflated sense of importance, so they will not waste their breath on a valid response or answer. Their answer is always the same and you can spot a Sgt. Schultz from a mile away. No matter what the question is or how it is phrased, they will answer with a simple, "I don't know." In other words, like Sgt. Schultz, they are telling you, "I know nothiiing...I see nothiiing!" Whenever I ask a person a question and they answer with "I don't know," I often wonder if they really know the answer but don't want me to know the answer. The way to get the proverbial Sgt. Schultz to change from "I don't know" to "I want you to know" is to feed his ego. He is hungry for self-promotion, so you must feed him and satisfy his narcissistic appetite.

I once interviewed a young thug carjacker that was arrested after he led police on a 100-mile car chase. He had kidnapped an elderly lady at knifepoint and then refused to slow the car down as she jumped to her escape from the passenger side. Every question that I asked the carjacker would get the same response of, "I don't know." Finally I decided to feed his ego and explained to him, "That was some fancy driving you did. You outran all those cops and turned grandma's car into a racing machine. You made that old Cadillac look like a Lamborghini. If it wasn't for the roadblock, you would be in Louisiana by now." Suddenly the carjacker went from not knowing to all-telling. He gave me great details of how he kidnapped the elderly lady and then drove her car like a madman. He proudly shared with me details of the robbery and gave a textbook confession. The case was so solid that the carjacker pled guilty and went to prison without attempting a plea bargain deal.

Sometimes people will say, "I don't know," and are telling the truth. To confirm that you are not dealing with a Sgt. Schultz type, ask a question that requires an obvious answer. For example, "What did you do today?" or "What color car were you driving?" If they say, "I don't know," to obvious questions, then you have a Sgt. Schultz type on your hands. You must feed the ego in order to get the mouth to open and say something truthful.

Another interview that I conducted was with a 21-year-old spoiled, rich kid that had shot and killed his friend after a night of drinking and dope smoking. He had never been held accountable for anything in his life and certainly would not respect any police authority. As I asked him questions about the shooting, his common and consistent answer was "I don't know." Finally, I explained to him, "You have a chance here to tell your side of the story. If you choose to go silent and be slaughtered like a lamb in the public's eye, then that is your decision and this interview is over." He had such rebellion in him that he would not even end the interview because it wasn't on his terms and didn't serve his agenda. He was emotionally torn between two decisions; he caught a vision of a slaughtered lamb and I had found the theme to connect to his emotional story. He began to ask me about going to court on the case, and who would testify against him. I explained to him that if he would not answer my questions, then neither would I answer his. At this point, I watched the pride-filled, rich kid humble himself and let go of his ego. His fear of the unknown became greater than his strength for withholding truthful information. He began to share with me details about the shooting; how it happened and why it happened. He left the interview room a different person from the arrogant punk that went into the interview room. He was resistant but actually relieved to tell the story.

Located in the Bible at Mark Chapter 11, Jesus handled some arrogant, pride-filled priests in the same manner as my interview with the spoiled rich kid. The Pharisee priests were trying to attack the character of Jesus, and began to ask him questions about his credentials. They wrongly assumed that Jesus would choke under pressure and would stumble over his own statements. The Pharisee Priests did not realize that they were talking to the King of kings that spoke the world into existence. Jesus invented speech and is the Creator of communication, so he would not be fooled by their foolishness. In Mark 11: 28 (TEV): They asked Jesus, "What right do you have to do these things?" He completely flanked them by stating, "First answer me and then I will answer you." Jesus asked, "Was John's baptism from Heaven or from men?" The Pharisee Priests discussed among themselves how they should answer Jesus because they didn't respect John or Jesus, but they knew the people did. In Mark 11:33 (TEV): They finally agreed that their politically correct answer should be "We don't know." Jesus simply said, "Neither will I answer you because you will not answer me." Notice that Jesus did not acknowledge the Pharisee's claim that they didn't know the answer to his question; he simply said that they would not answer his question. In other words, Jesus said, "If you choose to go silent and be slaughtered like lambs, that is your decision, but this interview is over!" The Pharisee Priests missed the Savior of the world because they wanted to condemn him rather than converse with him.

How much truth has been missed in interviews because we want to condemn someone, rather than comprehend someone. Even a cold- hearted serial killer has some truth to tell, so listen for it and receive it.

# THE NAME GAME

*(How the guilty talk using titles & names)*

# CHAPTER 6

———◆◉◆———

Growing up as a kid in Texas, I became bored easily. I began to use my creativity in negative ways. Most of my pranks were originals, so no law had been written against them yet. I invented schemes like dipping the tail of a neighbor's dog in paint; moving real estate signs around the community to places that were not for sale; and switching out my neighbor's egg laying hens for old broke down roosters. Needless to say, it wasn't pleasurable to live anywhere close to me as a kid. The older I grew, the more mischief I got into. My parents saw a problem and knew that an immediate intervention was needed.

At 15, I was sent to a military school in the middle of the desert in Roswell, New Mexico. This is the same school that helped build the young boy, Owen Wilson as he grew into a man and became a famous Hollywood actor. My parents knew that a strict, regimented environment would ensure that my every move would be monitored. They were hopeful that just maybe, some character would be built into me in the process. I met a lot of other characters just like me and quickly made friends with a rich and rowdy kid from Mexico City. His family owned a popular boot company that produced and imported boots to the U.S. His English was broken, but his spirit was not. All the cadets were forced to line up every morning at 5:00 a.m. in perfect military formation. A hot tempered and determined Italian drill instructor by the name of Sergeant Picasso would run us for hours around the barracks before breakfast. I realized that Sgt. Picasso had an artist name, but this guy could paint nothing but a picture of total exhaustion. After our endless miles of PT (physical training), Sgt. Picasso would line us up again in perfect formation and go down the line asking silly questions like, "Who's the Commander in Chief?" I knew who President Ronald Reagan was and could answer in English, but for the kid from Mexico City, it was a real challenge. Any cadet not having the correct answer would be subject to multiple push-ups. Sgt. Picasso would get angry and get in the face of the Mexican kid and demand an answer. The kid would answer the questions to the best of his ability with his limited English and would often say, "Forgive please, I no comprendo, Sergeanto Piaso!" The kid's language flowed with such sincerity and rhythm that Sgt. Picasso never realized the kid always mispronounced his name on purpose and changed it to "Piaso." I later learned from the kid that "Piaso" means clown in Spanish. For an entire year, Sgt. Picasso was being insulted and called a clown to his face but assumed that he had cadets shaking in their boots with fear.

Names are very important in the interview process. Every law enforcement interviewer needs to pay close attention to names and titles as people talk and tell a story. It is a common attempt among the guilty to dehumanize and devalue the victim by not giving them a name. The suspect wants to remain emotionally unattached, so he sees the victim as nameless and without value. During a highly publicized political investigation, a U.S. president was being interviewed about his involvement with infidelity while in the White House. This president was a former lawyer turned governor, and he had skyrocketed all the way to the Oval Office. He was very intelligent and had been trained in the power of his words through the interview process. However, even this well-trained and skilled lawyer choked and stumbled over his own statements as his deception was revealed and truth came out. The president looked straight in the face of America and confidently said,

"I want you to listen to me, I'm going to say this again... I did not have sexual relations with that woman!"

He then caught his own deception and quickly added her name. It was obvious that the president was lying because he had spent many hours with the woman, as she worked for him in the White House as an intern. He knew her personally, so he would also know her name personally. She was obviously more than just a "woman" to him, but he was attempting to dehumanize her as having no value or name.

Another prime example of the name game was an interview that I did with a killer in a cold case who murdered his pregnant wife in 2006. After years of different Homicide Detectives working the case and keeping it from falling through the cracks, we received new information from a new witness. The suspect was brought in and gave a self-serving admission that he had accidently broken his wife's neck and killed her in self-defense. She was very small in stature at five feet tall and one hundred pounds, so his self-defense theory was insulting. The suspect killed her in 2006, disposed of the body, and destroyed all physical evidence in the case. When an arrest was finally made in 2011 and the case was solved, he still refused to reveal the whereabouts of her body. I suspected that if we ever found her, there would be evidence of her being killed with a firearm because he was a gun enthusiast and even constructed homemade silencers in his home. The killer could not reveal the body because it would have revealed the truth and destroyed his self-defense theory. As I interviewed the suspect, I asked him to show us where his wife was buried so we could bring her body home and have a funeral. The suspect quickly dehumanized the victim without giving her a name and saying, "I don't know where it is, I went to go find it, but I couldn't find it again." The loyal wife and woman that he once claimed to love and cherish had now been demoted to an "It." The cold-hearted killer never revealed the location of his wife's body, so she was never found. However, murder charges were filed because of his detailed story of how he killed her and wrapped her up in trash bags with masking tape. He later accepted a plea bargain of 25 years without parole because of his recorded confession of the killing.

Located in the Bible at Genesis Chapter 4, God gives us an excellent example of the name game being played. It was the first murder in human history, and the first murderer avoided truth just like many others since him. Adam and Eve were the parents of two sons, Cain and Abel. The older son Cain became jealous of his little brother Abel, so Cain set the stage to kill Abel when no one was watching. Genesis 4:8 (HCSB) states, "Cain said to his brother Abel, lets go out to the field, and while they were in the field, Cain attacked his brother Abel and killed him." In Genesis 4:9 (HCSB), the Lord was interviewing Cain and asked "Where is your brother, Abel?" Notice that God used the victim's name as well as his title. God is allowing no wiggle room as Cain avoids a personal answer to a personal question. Cain's response to God's question give us a clue to his soul as he says, "I don't know. Am I my brother's keeper?" Cain is attempting to dehumanize and devalue the victim by not giving him a name. He had referred to Abel as "brother" and gave him a title, but not a name. Cain had disposed of his brother's body and thought that God would not find out. Cain wanted to stay far away from his brother's body just as he wanted to stay far away from his brother's name. Cain's statement of denial shows us when the guilty leave out the name, then the guilty leave out their shame.

During the interview process with people, look for repeated patterns where a name is left out and replaced with a title. It is perfectly acceptable if a mother refers to her child occasionally as "The baby" or a country boy refers to his wife as "The old lady." However, consistent patterns of "name" substitution shows deception. If you hear a relative say, "I didn't kill the baby" you should look for patterns of deception. If you hear a relative say, "I didn't kill Suzie Q" then expect a pattern of truth. Names are important to God because that is what defines us and gives us identity. Anything less takes away from the value of a person. I have often interviewed killers and will hear them make statements like "I know the lord butters my bread!" or "The man upstairs knows I'm innocent!" They are claiming Christianity without the Christ. They are using titles to replace a name, so there is nothing personal about their relationship with God. The guilty will often avoid the name of Jesus because they are trying to distance themselves from his truth. The guilty will treat Jesus like a victim from one of their crimes and stay far away. They will try to dehumanize and devalue Jesus by not giving our Lord and Savior a name.

# IS SILENCE GOLDEN OR
# JUST PLAIN YELLOW?

*(Getting past the strong silent type)*

# CHAPTER 7

———◈———

In the mid 1980's, I was a young rookie officer and assigned to the Houston City Jail on the night shift. My assignment was to walk the jail floor every twenty minutes to check on the welfare of those locked up. I recall walking and monitoring hundreds of prisoners along a narrow catwalk that ran parallel to the jail cells. On many occasions as I walked the jail floor, multiple prisoners would ask me various questions about charges being filed or courts being in session. One night as I walked past a particular jail cell, I observed a clean-cut white male in an impressive business suit sitting silently on his bed rack. He looked like he belonged in the board room of a great corporation but certainly not incarcerated in the pit of insanity. The male stared at me but said nothing, so I stopped and asked him why he was arrested. There was no answer, so I asked him his name. He continued his silence and stared, but said nothing. I figured that he wanted to remain anonymous, so

I respected his wishes and finished out my shift. The next night, I returned to work and started my shift by walking the jail again along the narrow catwalk. As I passed by the jail cells, I observed the same well-dressed white male sitting in the same place on his bunk. I stopped again and asked him about going to court. He maintained his silence once again and just stared at me. This time, I decided to check on the status of the silent prisoner and see what was happening with his case.

As I reviewed the booking information on the silent man, I learned that he was booked under the name of "Fnu Lnu." He had been in the city jail over 24 hours and was arrested by patrol officers for refusing to give his name and resisting arrest. "Fnu Lnu" is the common name given to people by police in Houston when their identity is in question. It is an acronym which stands for "First Name Unknown, Last Name Unknown." The silent man was found wandering through the streets of Houston causing a traffic pile up. Officers considered him uncooperative based upon his resistance and silence, so an arrest was made. Upon arrival at the jail, his fingerprints revealed nothing and his silence revealed nothing, so his identity was simply a mystery. I was told that he already been to court twice, but refused to answer the questions of the judge and was returned to his jail cell each time. After checking with the Houston Missing Persons Division, we discovered that the silent man had simply walked away from his father's funeral and had disappeared without contacting any family or friends. His father had been a well-known wealthy businessman, but the silent man wished to remain anonymous, so he sat in silence in the downtown jail. He had apparently experienced a mental breakdown over the death of his father. He had lost hope and lost his identity. He was released without charges and returned to recover with his family. The silent man would never have been arrested or put in jail if he would have only spoken the truth of who he was. Is silence golden or just plain yellow?

Every Sunday school class in America has used the story of Jonah and the whale to teach children in church. We have all heard the story of how Jonah refused to go where God told him to go, so God sent a great fish to swallow him up. Jonah was then vomited up by the great fish on the shore of the place where God told him to go in the first place. Jonah had become whale puke, so he finally agreed to do what God asked of him and preach in the city of Nineveh. After preaching to the people, Jonah became angry because there was a revival and 120,000 people turned from their sin and were saved. Maybe Jonah was afraid that Heaven might become overpopulated, and he didn't want any crazy neighbor's next to his mansion in Glory Land. In Jonah Chapter 4, God starts an interview process, but Jonah foolishly went from fish food to the Fifth Amendment. Jonah was mad, so he decided to remain silent with God and not answer any questions at all. In Jonah 4:4 (TEV), the Lord asked "What right do you have to be angry?" Verse 5 says, "Jonah went out east of the city and sat down." In other words, Jonah took his Fifth Amendment rights and refused to answer any questions, even from God. Now, let's study the strategy of God to see how the interview was handled when Jonah went silent. Our God, who had interviewed the greatest men in the Bible including Abraham, Isaac, and Israel was not intimidated by Jonah's silence. Our God, the great orator who had invented communication simply changed Jonah's atmosphere to change his attitude and get him to talk. The Bible says in Jonah 4:6-8 (TEV), "The Lord God made a plant grow up over Jonah to give him some shade, so that he would be more comfortable. Jonah was extremely pleased with the plant. But at dawn the next day, at God's command, a worm attacked the plant and it died. After the sun had risen, God sent a hot east wind, and Jonah was about to faint from the heat of the sun beating down on his head." Jonah wished he would die as he said "I am better off dead than alive." Notice that God used something as large as a whale or as small as a worm to entice Jonah to talk. God allowed Jonah to get comfortable in the shade, and then he allowed Jonah to get very uncomfortable in the sun. God used two extremes so the truth would begin to flow. He changed the atmosphere of Jonah to change the attitude of Jonah. In the last part of the book of Jonah, we see where God was able to get a confession from Jonah about his true feelings.

We as police investigators must play by the rules of the game according to constitutional rights, so we could never use heat exhaustion to get a confession. However, it is perfectly acceptable to buy lunch and feed someone some comfort food before an interview, where the proverbial heat will be turned up later. In the old days, it was called the "Good cop, bad cop strategy." We are literally bringing comfort to the subject before the discomfort begins with the subject. These two extremes help bring out the truth, and show the softness and the hardness of the velvet- covered brick. If someone is silent in the interview room, change their atmosphere to a place outside the interview room or even outside the police station. Sometimes, we must think outside the box, and take people outside the box for truth to be revealed.

My partner and I once drove a female suspect across Houston before she finally agreed to speak the truth and talk about the murder. She had shot and killed her boyfriend in a jealous rage and then tried to tamper with the crime scene to make it look like another woman was the killer. She would not open up in the interview room but began to tell the truth as we drove closer to her home searching for the pistol. The entire confession was recorded on my dash camcorder as she sat in the detective car in the driveway of her home. She was extremely embarrassed that the neighbors would see her and know what she did, so she told the truth to get out of there and get to jail faster. It was the extreme emotional contrast of being comfortable and then uncomfortable that cracked the hard coconut shell and allowed a confession to flow.

Sometimes during the interview process, people do not like the question, so they simply go silent and refuse to answer the question. The subject knows that if they answer the question, their innermost thoughts will be revealed, so they attempt to conceal the secret through silence. Just like the silent man sitting in the jail cell, some subjects will accept punishment and confinement rather than speak the truth and receive the relief of truth. I have discovered the best way to crack the code and break the silence in a suspect is to apply the same strategy that God applied with Jonah. Change the atmosphere of a suspect to change the attitude of a suspect. It does not require a whale, just a willingness to work outside the box.

# BIG HAT, NO CATTLE...
# BIG WORDS, NO CONTENT

*(How the guilty use words to cover up guilt)*

# CHAPTER 8

—————◈—————

Many years ago, my wife and I attended a country auction and I became intrigued by the chant and rhythm of the auctioneer. We had a place in the country, and we started attending different types of auctions to find good deals on cattle and farm equipment. All the items were sold to the highest bidder in rapid fire repetition as people competed to be the highest bidder. I knew there was a secret to this style of selling, so I attended an auctioneer school to learn the tricks of the trade. I planned to investigate and get inside the auction world to see how they succeeded to sell what some people considered to be just junk. In auctioneering school, it was explained to me that the auctioneer speaks very fast to create a sense of urgency with the buyers. In other words, the fast talking chant is psychological to inspire people to bid and buy and not miss out on the item being sold. It is a mental mind game being played at the auction house as people start bidding. Psychologists refer to this theory as "social proof;" if the majority of people are doing something, then it must be right and everyone wants to get involved. This is why people will wait in long lines for hours or even days to buy a product, because if others want something, they want it too. People will often start bidding on what other people have bid on, so it creates a shark frenzy of bidding in the crowd. This is why the auctioneer starts low and quickly raises the numbers as people jump in to bid. Most auctioneers are honest and simply use the energy of the crowd to make the sale.

However, after graduating from auctioneer school, I discovered some dishonest strategies used at some auctions. I went to an estate auction where old antiques and farm implements were being sold. As I stood in the back of the barn, I watched in amazement as the auctioneer worked the crowd like a cheap fiddle. As each item came up for bid, the auctioneer would start the rhythm of his chant. I listened carefully at the words that he was saying in rapid fire procession. He would start the bidding with something like "50 dollar where? I'm at 50 dollar here, now 50 dollar where? Will ya give me 50 dollar? Anywhere 50 dollar? Teddy bear 50 dollar, anywhere 50 dollar? Thank ya sir, now 60 dollar where?" The shrewd auctioneer was making a deceptive statement that the item was selling for 60 dollars and that he actually had bids at 50 dollars. The truth was that not one person in the crowd had even bid yet, and the first real bidder did not get on board until the bidding reached over 100 dollars. If an item did not get any real bids, the auctioneer would simply close the bidding at a fake price with a fake ghost bidder. He would quickly move to the next item before anyone realized that items had imaginary bids and bidders that did not exist. The dishonest auctioneer was simply talking fast and using filler words to create a sense of truth in his false statements. Many times, an item would start selling at 10 dollars and rapidly rise to 150 dollars, but only one or two buyers at the auction were even interested in bidding on the item. The auctioneer was using needless and useless filler words like "anywhere, teddy bear," and "thank ya sir" to create a sense of truth in his statements. His repeated rapid-fire filler words had fooled the crowd and people were being misled in large numbers.

As you interview subjects, listen carefully for the unneeded filler words in false statements. Some people will attempt deception by filling their sentences with words that are not needed. One example is:

Q: "Were you at the park during the shooting?"

A: "I really wasn't much there."

The word "really" is unneeded and implies "truly." When someone says "truly or honestly" at the beginning of their statement, expect deception from that person. They are trying to portray truth without saying the truth. The word "much" is also unneeded and does nothing to help the content of the sentence. It actually creates confusion by implying that the person may have been there, just not much. Another example is:

Q: "Where is the gun?"

A: "You know, I actually never saw a gun."

Once again we see unneeded filler words to create deception as the question was never answered. The most logical answer should be, "I don't know." The interviewer asked "Where" but the subject avoids answering "Where." Just because he never saw the gun doesn't excuse him from knowing where the gun is. The phrase "You know" implies "obviously," and the word "actually" implies "truly" and both are unneeded in the sentence. No truthful English speaker would ever use an awkward sentence like "Obviously, truly, I never saw a gun." Once again it shows that someone is trying to portray truth without saying the truth. These phrases are similar to the dishonest auctioneer trying to fill his sentences with useless words and sell a broke down donkey at a quarter-horse auction.

Many times in the Homicide Division, we would nickname the killers in our cases for simplicity of identity. Lawrence became "Scary Larry" and William became "Chilly Billy." I heard of ranchers in Montana doing the same thing by calling a dangerous grizzly bear "Teddy the Terror." When killers act like beast, they get named like beast. I was assigned a murder case where the suspect was accused of shooting and killing the victim in a robbery. The suspect's first name was Raymond, but he was quickly given the nickname "Boom-A-Ray" because of the repetitive filler word that he used while speaking. The following is an example of what Boom-A-Ray said;

"We were chilling at the crib, and BOOM, them girls showed up. We were going to hang out, but BOOM, they scat and took off walking. I didn't see no dude get shot, cause BOOM, I was just chilling and not tripping!"

Every few seconds, Boom-A-Ray would use the filler word "BOOM" in his statements; it was very hard to follow the flow of his communication. After hours of interviewing, Boom-A-Ray finally admitted that he was involved in the robbery and murder of an innocent man. I found it interesting as Boom-A-Ray talked about the shooting and the gun going off, the word "BOOM" suddenly and mysteriously disappeared from his vocabulary. The only time in the entire interview that the word "BOOM" would have been appropriate, but Boom-A-Ray left it out.

A biblical example of filler words being used to hide deception comes from the devil himself. Jesus tells us about the character of the devil in John 8:44 (HCSB): "He was a murderer from the beginning and has not stood in the truth, because there is no truth in him. When he tells a lie, he speaks from his own nature because he is a liar and the father of liars." When Jesus said that the devil was a murderer and liar from the beginning, he is speaking about what happened from the first book in the Bible, Genesis, which means "beginning." In Genesis Chapter 3, we see Adam and Eve in the Garden of Eden. The devil sees an opportunity to attack humanity, so he starts a casual conversation with Eve. The devil arrives in the form of a serpent; since Eve lives in a zoo and is married to the world's first zookeeper, she is not startled to see a snake. The devil tries to confuse Eve about what God had told them and begins to distort God's truth. God had placed Adam and Eve in a beautiful garden and allowed them to eat from all the endless varieties of fruit trees, but advised them to not eat from one specific tree. God advised Adam and Eve that if they ate the forbidden fruit, they would die. Eve was naïve and assumed that she could convince the devil of what God had said, but Satan quickly twisted the truth and confused her. Eve explained to the devil in Genesis 3:2-3 (NKJV): "And the woman said to the serpent, we may eat the fruit of the trees of the garden, but of the fruit of the tree which is in the midst of the garden, God has said, You shall not eat it nor touch it, lest you die." At this point, the devil saw his opportunity and attacked with his words to deceive Eve in verse 4 (NKJV), "Then the serpent said to the woman, you will not SURELY die!" Did you notice how the devil used an unneeded filler word to portray truth without saying the truth? The word "surely" sounds positive but does nothing to help the meaning of the statement and actually hinders the content of the sentence.

The devil is an expert at saying something negative and spinning it as a positive. He wears a big hat but has no cattle, so he is a counterfeit and a fake. Unfortunately, the devil is still using this same strategy today. We all know the story's sad ending. Adam and Eve ate the forbidden fruit and allowed sin, disease, and destruction to run rampant through humanity.

# ORDER & DISORDER
# IN THE COURT

*(The sequence of events tell secrets)*

# CHAPTER 9

———⇒◉⇐———

As a young police officer first starting my career, I often found myself getting subpoenas to court on minor cases such as traffic violations. I once spent an entire day in a jury trial for a red light violation, and thought I was God's gift to law enforcement. After several years of routine traffic court, I decided to expand my horizons and pursue something other than the simple misdemeanors. I decided to attend a latent fingerprint school and learn how to recover criminal prints from crime scenes. I found this new job messy but rewarding as I would fling fingerprint dust all over cars, houses, or any other object that a suspect might have touched. I often would look like a West Virginia Coal Miner after leaving a crime scene, but identified many crooks from fingerprints.

Late one night, patrol officers received a call about a female victim who had been found locked in the trunk of her own vehicle. The suspects had car-jacked the lady from her driveway earlier in the evening and taken all her credit cards. They didn't want the lady to report the car or the credit cards stolen, so they tossed her in the trunk of the car as they drove around all night using her credit cards. The lady told the story of being terrified as the suspects drove her car recklessly across curbs and through back-alley speed bumps. The lady assumed that she would not survive the experience so actually wrote her family a "Goodbye" note on a napkin using lip stick. After running out of beer and cigars, the suspects decided to stop at a convenience store and restock their party supplies. As the suspects went inside the store, the lady saw an opportunity, so she began to scream and pound on the trunk with her fists. Several people in the parking lot were passing by and heard the commotion coming from the trunk. As a small crowd of people gathered around the trunk of the car, the suspects realized their scheme was about to be exposed. They simply slipped away from the store and slithered into the darkness of the night. Patrol officers arrived and were able to release the lady unharmed from the trunk of her own car. I arrived on the scene and was able to recover the most perfect right hand print from the outer lid of the trunk. It seems that one of the suspects carelessly slammed the trunk closed as the lady was violently tossed inside. Afterwards, they put on gloves to avoid leaving fingerprints on the interior of her car. The order in which they conducted their crime caused them to get caught.

After several setbacks and resets from the court system, the kidnapping case would finally go to trial. The case went to court and the right hand print that I had recovered from the trunk would be the key piece of evidence. I testified for the very first time in a felony case and felt more like I was working for God, rather than being an arrogant rookie in the traffic court. From this case, I learned humility as I felt such strong compassion for the victim. The lady was allowed to read her napkin note to the jury, which she had written from the trunk of her own car. After a three day trial, the defendant was found guilty and stood before the judge for his sentencing phase. The defendant became impatient and began to ask how many years in prison should he expect. The judge stared in silence at the defendant as he chose his words carefully. He came back with the perfect answer at the perfect time. The judge told the defendant "So you want to know how many years you will serve in prison? Just know that your parole officer has not even been born yet."

The order in which a crook commits his crime will often cause the truth to be revealed. Remember, the kidnapper put on his gloves after touching the car, so his prints told the story of the crime. The order in which a crook describes his crime will also cause the truth to be revealed. In the Bible at the book of First Kings, we see an excellent example of the order of events showing truth. In 1 Kings 3, King Solomon was a great king in Jerusalem and the wisest man that ever lived. The Bible says that God gave Solomon wisdom, so there has never been anybody like him and there will never be again. As the king over Israel, Solomon often had to do double duty as a judge and make decisions in a courtroom. On one occasion, two prostitutes came to the king and stood before him. The prostitutes explained how they were roommates and both had newborn babies. In 1 Kings 3:18-21 (NKJV) one of women explained, "Then it happened, the third day after I had given birth, that this woman also gave birth. And we were together, no one was with us in the house, except the two of us in the house. And this woman's son died in the night because she lay on him. So she arose in the middle of the night and took my son from my side while your maidservant slept, and laid him in her bosom and laid her dead child in my bosom. And when I rose in the morning to nurse my son, there he was, dead. But when I had examined him in the morning, indeed, he was not my son whom I had borne."

The woman gave her testimony to the king and then the two women began to speak and cross examine each other. Notice how the order of importance is utilized in their statements in verse 22, "No. But the living one is my son and the dead one is your son." And the other woman said, "No. But the dead one is your son and the living one is my son, thus they spoke before the king." Solomon began to evaluate and look very closely into the two women's statements in verse 23, "And the king said, the one says, this is my son who lives, and your son is the dead one, and the other says, No, but your son is the dead one and my son is the living one." At this point, Solomon knew who was speaking truth and who was speaking trash by analyzing the two statements. Solomon had noticed that the true mother of the live baby mentioned the live baby first and then mentioned the dead baby last. The true mother of the dead baby mentioned the dead baby first and the live baby last. People will mentally put in order what is most important to them. People will speak in order of importance as well to show what's important to them by putting first things first. The woman of the dead baby had the death weighing heavy on her heart, so death was mentioned before life.

King Solomon already knew the truth but wanted to show the courtroom the truth, so he created physical evidence for the courtroom to see. He advised his soldiers to take a sword and cut the baby in half and give each woman one half of the baby. At this point, the true mother of the live child spoke up and told the woman with the dead child to keep the baby. The woman with the living child would rather see her baby alive with the other woman, than be killed in her own possession. Love will always outlast a lie, and Solomon knew it. That is why he had given the order to divide and dispense the baby, in order for truth to come out. In the end, King Solomon ordered the live baby be returned to the rightful mother and not be killed. The deceitful mother had put on a proverbial glove to cover her lie, but unknowingly left a fingerprint of deceit. CSI Solomon found the evidence and used it against her.

# PRONOUNS CAN
# ANNOUNCE THE CRIME

*(How the guilty take possession of their crimes)*

# CHAPTER 10

———— ◆ ————

Every police officer has crazy testimonies to tell. No one can be involved in law enforcement long without collecting a series of strange stories. I remember many bizarre things happening while I worked the city jail, but one story stands out in my memory. One busy night, I was assigned to the jail lock-up tank and I heard the voices of men yelling from a cell located at the end of the catwalk. I went immediately to investigate the loud voices and arrived within seconds in front of the jail cell. As I peered into the cell expecting to see a crowd, I noticed that only one man was occupying the cell. He stood in the middle of the cell and stared at me with crazy eyes. I asked him the obvious question of "Who was yelling?" The man pointed towards the wall behind him and said, "They all were yelling!" I realized that he was in the cell alone so I dismissed him as a crazy nut-job, but I was still baffled about hearing multiple voices. As I walked away from his cell, I once again heard the voices of several men yelling from the cell.

I assumed that either my eyes or my ears were playing tricks on me, so I decided to get a closer look. I opened the cell door and went inside with the lone man standing like a statue in the middle of his cell. As I walked into the jail cell with the man, he quickly held up his arms up as if holding back a crowd and said, "Stand back, there's not room for all of us in here!" I explained to the confused man that jail overcrowding was not a problem in his cell as he was all alone. The disillusioned man began to yell out in several tones and voices and I realized that he was either an amazing impressionist or demon possessed. It was an unusual event to hear the multiple voices coming from just one man. The man was using lots of pronouns like "us, we," and "they" but his story of multiple offenders was quickly losing its credibility. I decided to get him out of the jail with the first jail court docket leaving, where a much wiser magistrate could make a ruling on multiple offenders with only one man present.

One U.S. president that prided himself as a Harvard Lawyer was being questioned about his wrong-doing and cover-up in the White House. He answered by saying, "Mistakes were made and we misjudged the outcome." From a distance it looked as if he was admitting to making a mistake. However, he never said "I made a mistake" or "I misjudged the outcome." He never took possession, ownership, or responsibility for making a mistake. He plainly stated "we misjudged" so he is not taking full responsibility for what happened, even though he is Commander in Chief and made the ultimate decision. The president was being deceptive in saying "we" instead of "I" because misery loves company and doesn't want to be alone in being wrong. Deception can be detected in a jail house nut-job or a finely pressed and polished president.

Pronouns are very important in determining truth in statements or determining if a statement is misleading. If someone is using pronouns such as "us, we, they," or "ours" in their statements, then we can be sure that they are saying that more than one person is involved. Look for signs of deception where a person uses a singular pronoun like "me" and then later changes it to a plural pronoun like "we." Some people don't want to carry the burden of blame alone. There is safety in numbers and misery loves company. Sometimes, there is deception like the nut-job in the jail cell that imagined the company of others, or the president that imagined others were also at fault, so played the blame game.

Pronouns show possession so if a person says "my gun, my car, or my bedroom" then it will show that these items are personal possessions. If someone says "My car is parked in the parking lot" then the car is seen as the possession, but the parking lot is not.

I once interviewed a girlfriend that stabbed her boyfriend to death and then called 911 to claim self-defense. She explained it by saying "He walked into my bedroom to attack me so I ran to the kitchen." The two lived together and slept in the same bedroom, but she claimed her possession of it by saying "my" bedroom and not "our" bedroom. Notice how the bedroom was hers, but not the kitchen. She went on to tell me, "I grabbed one of my knives from the kitchen and went back to my bedroom." Once again, notice the pronouns announcing her knife and her bedroom as possessions. As the girlfriend talked about the stabbing of the boyfriend in the bedroom, she said, "He was going to attack me so I stabbed him with the knife." She proclaimed it as "her knife" in the kitchen, but now she had changed it to "the knife" as the stabbing took place in the bedroom. She wanted to distance herself from possession so changed it from "my knife" to "the knife" to deceitfully cover up the murder. Her claims of self-defense quickly fell apart as blood from the dead boyfriend was found deceitfully covered up by the sheets in the bed. With a knife sticking out of his chest and lying dead on the floor, the boyfriend was the only one with a right to claim self-defense to save his life.

If someone is repeatedly saying "my" in a statement and then changes it to "the" later, then expect deception and look for the lie. For example:

Q: "Where were you last night?"

A: "I was at MY apartment."

Q: "Was Suzie Q with you?"

A: "No, she was not at THE apartment."

*Another example:

Q: "Whose car is this?"

A: "This is MY car."

Q: "Are there drugs in your car?"

A: "There aint no drugs in THE car!"

When the pronouns of "my, me," and "I" suddenly lose possession of a property, then expect deception and know that you are on the trail of a guilty conscience. In a crazy, proverbial way, killers will suddenly lose possession of knives, drug dealers suddenly lose possession of cars, and people will suddenly lose possession of any property that brings them close to their guilt.

# THE PATH TO THE
# PATHOLOGICAL LIAR

*(Understanding lies & the people that love them)*

# CHAPTER 11

If you have ever taken a breath of life as a human being, then you have made an untrue statement sometime during your life. All people have lied in some way to protect their interest or the interests of others. Thankfully, most people do not make it a habit to mislead others and actually feel bad about making a false statement. However, for the habitual liar, it often starts as a child and runs through their senior years in all cultures, genders, and ethnic backgrounds. A little boy was asked by his mother about the fresh baked cookies that were missing.

Q: "Did you eat the cookies?"

A: "No mom, I didn't eat one."

Q: "Well that's funny, there's only one left."

A: "That's the one I didn't eat."

Sounds comical, but this little liar will sharpen his skills of deception over time as more cookies go missing. Today he conquers a cookie jar, tomorrow he conquers your credit report. Some people will twist truth, stretch truth, and withhold truth in order to shine the best possible light on themselves. Most people that choose to tell a lie, believe that they will not get caught. No one in their right mind would make an untrue statement knowing that their lie would be uncovered and found out later. However, a pathological liar is a different animal and not in his right mind. The pathological liar will make an untrue statement today to accomplish his goal, knowing that the truth will come out at a later date. Pathological liars are rare but often tell a lie when the lie does not even benefit them, and the truth would just as easily work. The word "pathos" means suffering a disease and pathological liars have a disease to spread as they spew their lies to anyone who will listen.

One U.S. president was trying to convince a nation that his health care package was in the best interest of the American people. He switched from president to salesman by trying to sell a clunker for cash. He made the following statement many times in many different public speeches.

"We will keep this promise to the American people. If you like your doctor, you can keep your doctor, period!"

This statement was made by a pathological liar that knew his statements were false and would be discovered false once his agenda was achieved. We have all been infuriated by the lies of a pathological liar as they seem so convincing and so sincere at the time, and yet we feel stupid for believing them. The pathological liar is not concerned with your level of intelligence as it is not about you, but only about him. His ego is larger than life and his perceived intelligence is far superior to everyone else's, so he sells the story knowing that it will be discredited later. When caught in the lie, the pathological liar will simply tell another lie on top of the lie to cover up the original lie. The following is a funny story that explains it well. A wife comes home to find her husband in bed with another woman. The nude husband throws the sheets over the nude woman and climbs out of bed saying, "What are you going to believe honey, your lying eyes or what I am about to tell you?" Even when caught with his pants down, the pathological liar will never come clean.

A good example of a pathological liar in the Bible can be found in Acts Chapter 5. A married couple named Ananias and Sapphira sold some land and went public about bringing all the proceeds from the sale to the church. The fact that they were bringing an offering to the church and giving something to God was a good thing, but the bragging would bring them down. They informed the church that all of the proceeds were brought to the church, when they actually withheld part of the proceeds from the sale. As Peter was a leader in the church, he held the couple accountable to truth and interviewed them separately. Every police investigator should learn from Peter and never interview more than one person at a time and always separately. The husband was interviewed first but he would not get honest, even though evidence testified against him. The wife was interviewed second and the conversation was documented in verse 8 (TEV) as Peter said to her, "Tell me, was this the full amount you and your husband received for your property?" Even with her husband already interrogated and found out, Sapphira stuck to the script and would not change her story.

Peter wanted Sapphira to be truthful so he even offered her an escape from her untrue statement, but she would simply not get honest. The Bible says that both her and her husband fell dead and went to the grave with their lies. There is a clear scripture that explains why pathological liars cling to their lies. It is all based on a prideful attitude and a narcissistic personality disorder, so we know what will happen to them in the end. It is found in Proverbs 16:18 (NKJ), "Pride goes before destruction, a haughty spirit before the fall." The fall can be physical, spiritual, financial, emotional, or through credibility, but it will come.

# BUILD YOUR CASE LIKE CONCRETE STEPS

*(Building your case by building your questions)*

# CHAPTER 12

———⊶◈⊷———

Concrete is the best known substance in construction to hold up the weight of a structure, so it is often used in the foundation at the start of a building project. Concrete also serves as a barrier to contain large amounts water, as one pound of concrete can hold back hundreds of pounds of water. Concrete is a simple substance made from sand, gravel, Portland cement and mixed with water. As concrete is poured, it goes through a three step process that takes it from a liquid to a solid form. The first phase is "soft" where the concrete is filled with fluid and mostly unstable. The second phase is "setting" where the concrete is in the process of drying so can be smoothed to the desired shape. The third phase is "stable" where the concrete is cured and set in the final shape it will take. Once the concrete is stable and cured, it can hold water or hold up a foundation. The interview process can be compared to the setting of concrete, where initially the case won't hold water and won't hold up in a courtroom. Our job as investigators is to get the case from soft, to setting, and ultimately to stable where it is set in stone.

As police investigators, we must ask specific questions to get specific answers. We build our case very methodically, with each individual question as we take one step at a time. Never answer your question as you ask your question, as it puts a predetermined assumption in the interview process. This method allows the suspect to simply agree with you so his answer remains soft, and the truth can be easily avoided. I call it the "Fuzzy-Wuzzy" method where the children's poem gives the answer within the question. It goes:

"Fuzzy-Wuzzy was a bear.

Fuzzy-Wuzzy had no hair.

Fuzzy-Wuzzy wasn't fuzzy, was he?"

It sounds ridiculous and no detective would intentionally ask such crazy questions, but sometimes an answer within the question makes it appear like a Fuzzy-Wuzzy moment. You want no fluid answers in your interviews that have the consistency of soft concrete changing its shape. Here are examples of bad interviewing questions:

Q: "You didn't stab her did you?"

Q: "You don't expect me to believe that do you?"

Q: "You don't have a weapon do you?"

Q: "You don't know where the body is, do you?"

The following questions are good direct questions that require a direct answer and allow for no wiggle room by the suspect. For example:

Q: "Did you stab her?"

Q: "How can you explain it where people will believe it?"

Q: "Do you have a weapon?"

Q: "Where is the body?"

As you ask the direct question, get on their level and look straight into their eyes and wait for their response. Remember, you are waiting for the spirit to pull the soul towards the truth so it may take time. I have waited up to a minute in silence before the truth was presented or some trash was attempted. Sometimes silence is golden, and sometimes it is just plain yellow. Occasionally, detectives are so excited that a suspect is actually talking to them that they get into a hurry and ask compound questions (two questions in one sentence). This method allows the suspect to throw confusion in an interview by answering one question and avoiding the other, or answering both with one answer. The following are examples:

Q: "Have you ever been in a gang or hung out with Clyde?"

Q: "Did you ever threaten your girlfriend or hurt her?"

Q: "Do you have a gun or other weapons?"

As these compound questions are presented, the suspect can honestly answer "yes or no" and the detective will not know which question has been answered. If a suspect is being deceptive, usually they will choose the part of the question that can be answered honestly and use great detail to explain it. For example:

A: "Honestly, I was raised in a bad neighborhood so I actually saw a lot of gangs doing a lot of bad stuff. I mean, I wasn't into the gang scene so I avoided them and got involved in school activities. You know, I always tried to be a loner and pretty much kept to myself."

Notice how the suspect uses great detail with lots of filler words to talk about gangs, and appears to completely answer the question. However, the suspect leaves out the subject of "Clyde" entirely so he has avoided the second question altogether. The suspect may have spent every day with Clyde, but he tells us that he "tried to be a loner." Trying to do something is different than actually doing it. Remember, one question at a time and one step at a time to build the concrete steps.

Occasionally suspects will not answer a question with a simple "yes or no" but want to explain every answer. It could be deception or just the nervousness of talking about a traumatic event. Some detectives get frustrated and try to shut them up so the next question can be answered. I allow for some rambling of words because I figure if I give them enough proverbial rope, then they will eventually hang themselves. I have the best shot at a confession as the conversation is flowing, so why not wade through some trash in order to get to the truth. Remember that soft answers will eventually turn into stable and hardened concrete answers, but we must allow the curing process to take place. Keep them talking because silent suspects never give confessions. If a suspect starts to say something but then waits and hesitates, you must keep the flow of communication going. You take the lead in the conversation by saying something like "Then what happened?" or "I'm listening!" or "Go on!" to remind him that he has committed to a statement.

I was assigned a suspicious suicide case where a dead man was found asphyxiated in a low rent motel room. His body was hung up about four feet from the floor, where his neck was tied by a cord from a horizontal electrical conduit. The leading methods of suicide are gunshots and hangings, but I had seen strangulations that were staged to look like suffocations in previous cases. The motel room almost appeared to be a staged suicide scene as the ligature around the victim's neck seemed arranged and orchestrated. The suicide note did not seem authentic either, as it was vague and written on the mirror with a bar of soap, even though pens and paper were present. The victim appeared to have a good job and a good future, so the suicide was being questioned. After looking at recorded security cameras, one well-known prostitute was seen coming out of the victim's motel room about 12 hours before the body was discovered by employees. After several weeks of ducking and dodging the police, the prostitute was located and interviewed in the Homicide Division. Her choice of occupation meant that she avoided the police daily, and not just because of a possible murder investigation. The girl kept trying to convince me that she was of no value to the case and had not taken part in the death of the man. She rambled on and on telling me various stories about her life and giving great details of her sexually oriented business operations. She eventually admitted to spending time with the victim in the motel room and even admitted being paid by the victim. The prostitute continued to try to convince me that the victim was alive and well when she left his motel room. She said that the victim appeared depressed because he told her that he had asked a girl named Irene to marry him, but the girl declined his offer. The victim had also told the prostitute that all women in his life had rejected him, except those being paid for their time. I knew that the prostitute was the last person in the motel room and the last person to see the victim alive. Based on video security camera evidence, if a killing took place, then she would be the killer.

After allowing the girl to be long-winded and ramble on about insignificant issues, she suddenly cleared the case with just one simple sentence. She said, "He showed me an engagement ring that he had paid over $1200.00 dollars for, so I know this Irene girl rejected him." What the prostitute didn't know was that we did find a diamond engagement ring in the motel room with the victim. Any prostitute in her right or wrong mind would have taken the engagement ring from the victim after killing him, and never mention the ring to the police. Robbery would have been her motive for killing him, so she would never leave an expensive ring behind. We later found the receipt for the ring and found the mystery girl named Irene to confirm the story of the rejected victim and his suicidal threats. It seems that his broken heart led to a broken neck as he hung himself in a lonely motel room on the low side of town.

This is a classic case of allowing someone to ramble in conversation, and either clearing or convicting themselves with words. The prostitute certainly left enough evidence at the motel to get a court of law to convict her in a murder case. The DNA, fingerprints, and motel security cameras all pointed to her as the killer in this case. I was giving her enough proverbial rope to hang herself in the interview as I felt that she had hung the victim. However, her rambling of words cleared her as a killer and showed that a true suicide took place, but not a murder case.

# THINGS THAT MAKE
# YOU GO...HMM?

*(Asking the right questions to get the right answers)*

# CHAPTER 13

———⟫⟨⟨⟩⟩⟪———

I have a cute little granddaughter that is just learning to speak the English language. She is just learning the sounds that all the animals make so she tries to imitate their sounds. She knows that the cow goes "moo" and the dog goes "ruff" and the llama goes "hmm." We actually have llamas on our country farm so she learned the sound through hearing them up close and personal. The llama is an inquisitive animal that often hums as he investigates to satisfy his curiosity. As we learn things in life, we as curious people also hear things that make us go "hmm." My granddaughter is learning new words every day and increasing her vocabulary with every experience. She constantly tries to put words together so she can express her thoughts, desires, and wishes in a simple method of communication. She will say things like "I mad" if she is upset or "I jump" if she is happy and wants to express her emotions.

Every question that I ask her is received like the most important question ever asked of her. If I ask her if she wants a certain toy that she really likes, then she will answer quickly and directly in the positive without hesitation. If I ask her a question that she doesn't like, then she will also answer quickly and directly in the negative without hesitation. I once asked her for a donut that she was eating and she quickly told me, "No!" My granddaughter wants the truth of her feelings to be known quickly and directly and without hesitation. She wants the truth to be portrayed and not delayed or miscommunicated in any way. She is just a toddler learning more every day, so any questions asked of her are serious and taken with the upmost importance. No one had ever asked her for a donut before so she took the question very seriously and gave me the answer fast.

Most people reach adulthood and become experts at communication; for them, speaking becomes very routine. After years of talking, they have been asked millions of questions, and have become desensitized by the flood of questions coming in. If you order food at a fast food restaurant, you will be asked about ten questions before you taste a single French fry. However, most people in society today have never been asked if they killed someone or if they committed a violent crime like a home invasion. Just as my toddler granddaughter knows, the question is serious so the answer should be serious as well. The communication should be clear and quick and not miscommunicated in any way. If it is the first time that someone asked you for a donut or the first time that someone asked you about a murder, you should take the question seriously and answer it directly.

People that want truth to be told will answer quickly and directly, especially when they may lose something like their freedom by miscommunicating the wrong answer. The most obvious answer if someone accuses you of a crime that you did not commit should be a quick and decisive "No, I did not!" When people attempt to add useless words to very serious answers, then we as police investigators should expect deception. We need to ask follow-up questions to clarify if they are just unsure or actually trying to be deceptive.

Q: "Do you know where the gun is?"

A: "I couldn't tell you!"

This answer shows signs of deception as the suspect tells us that he couldn't tell us the answer. If he did tell, then truth might be revealed. The correct response should be, "No" or "I don't know."

Q: "Did you shoot Suzie Q?"

A: "I could never shoot anybody!"

This answer shows signs of deception because we are not talking about anybody, we specifically asked about Suzie Q. We asked a specific question but received a vague answer. The suspect is trying devalue the victim by taking away the name of the victim. The correct response should be "No," or "I did not shoot Suzie Q."

Q: "Did you shoot Clyde?"

A: "Absolutely not!" or "Of course not!"

These answers shows signs of deception because the suspect is attempting the same tricks as the devil in Genesis 3:4 of the Bible. A positive filler word is put in front of a negative word to bring validity to the answer. The correct response should be "No," or "I did not."

Q: "Do you know who fired the gun?"

A: "I wouldn't know!"

This answer shows signs of deception because the suspect is actually saying if he had a choice to know, then he would choose not to know. The correct response should be "No," or "I don't know."

Q: "Are you sure about the shooter?"

A: "I'm 100% positive about him!"

This answer shows signs of deception because numbers are infinite and can go on forever. 100 % positive may only be 10% sure if it is based on 1000% ratio. It is common for people to say they are 99% or 1000% positive and still be completely wrong.

Q: "Did you take Bonnie from her house?"

A: "I loved her too much to do that!"

This answer shows signs of deception because people will attempt to inject their feelings without injecting the truth. They may feel love for someone after the abduction and after the anger wears off, so now they regret it. The correct response should be "No," or "I did not."

Q: "Did you kill Clyde?"

A: "I couldn't hurt anybody!"

This answer shows signs of deception because we never asked about hurting Clyde, we asked about killing him. If death was instant then Clyde may have not felt pain or suffering. Also, Clyde was not just anybody, he was the victim. The suspect portrayed the truth without saying the truth.

When people start their sentences with "I wouldn't" or "I couldn't" to answer a question, then expect deception in their answer. By giving these responses, they are only telling you things that they "shouldn't" do, but not actual things that they did. As police officers, we ask questions of victims, witnesses, and suspects and sometimes an answer given sounds odd and out of place. If you ask a question and the response doesn't seem to fit the question and it makes you go...hmm, then dig deeper for the truth. The following statements were given as suspicious responses that don't quite fit the questions or fully explain the truth:

Q: "Did you go to the club?"

A: "Well, I certainly never intended to."

Intentions change like freshly poured concrete. What someone intends to do today may change tomorrow. Investigate further because this answer tells us nothing.

Q: "Who do you think killed him?"

A: "I am confident that it was Clyde."

Confidence changes like intentions. Never rely on someone's changing confidence to build your case. Investigate further to see why they are confident.

Q: "Who do you think shot him?"

A: "All I can say is that it wasn't me."

"All I can say" means that I have more to say but I am withholding something. Investigate further because this answer tells us nothing.

Q: "Who stole the car?"

A: "All I know is that someone drove away."

"All I know" means that I have limited knowledge and limited involvement in the case. Investigate further to see what else they know, and who is this mysterious someone?

Q: "Did you go to the park?"

A: "You know, I went there a long time ago."

"You know" means that it is obvious to me and should be obvious to you also. The person is telling you that perhaps there is more that you should know. Investigate further to find the truth.

Q: "Did you get into an argument with her?"

A: "No, I mean, she knew me a long time and we never fought."

"I mean" means that my answer just changed so my words and my thoughts line up now. I can't tell you what I really mean.

Q: "Were you a faithful husband?"

A: "I always tried to be faithful to her."

Trying to do something means that I have not accomplished it yet, so there may have been failed attempts.

Q: "Were you faithful as a wife?"

A: "I think I was faithful to him."

To "think" means that I believe it but others may not. Our thoughts are subject to change just like freshly poured concrete, so nothing is solid or stable enough to stand on.

Q: "Did you see the car in the alley?"

A: "So, I walked by there but didn't actually see a car."

When a sentence is started with "So," then get ready for a well-thought-out story. The person has prepared, practiced, and perfected the story.

The following is an actual interview that took place on a morning show between a news journalist and a suspected wife killer. On Christmas Eve, the pregnant wife disappeared so the husband quickly appeared all over national television. He was a person of interest, so he used the media to portray himself as someone who cared and wanted to find his missing wife and unborn son.

Q: "What kind of marriage was it?"

A: "God... The first word that comes to mind is YOU KNOW, glorious. I MEAN we took care of each other, very well. She WAS amazing. She IS amazing."

Q: "You haven't mentioned your son?"

A: "THAT WAS... IT IS so hard. I can't go in there. The door is closed until there's SOMEONE to put in there."

There are more red flags than flag poles can hold to this interview where the suspect is revealing his guilt about killing his wife and unborn son. The husband's soul wants to confess so badly, but his flesh is holding him back. He is busting at the seams to tell the truth, but the hard shell of humanity just won't allow the sweet truth to flow. Several times, he refers to his wife and child in the past tense even though their bodies weren't found for another four months. Notice how he devalues the unborn baby by calling him "someone" but not mentioning Baby Conner's name. The cold hearted killer husband will now be spending every Christmas until he dies sitting on California death row.

I recall the murder of a man found beaten to death in the middle of his own living room floor. There were no suspects, witnesses, or murder weapon at the apartment when the police arrived, so the investigation started from scratch. As Homicide Detectives arrived on the scene, we looked around the apartment and noticed strange indentions in the living room ceiling above where the victim had been killed. The sheet rock in the ceiling had about 20 perfectly uniformed indentions in the shape of the letter "T." This is one of those moments in life that makes you go…hmm. Like the inquisitive llama, we just stumbled onto something. What object consistently makes the letter "T" each and every time it strikes a surface? Any Texan worth his weight in barbeque sauce could immediately identify the object as a metal "T" post used in barbed wire fencing. The suspect had brought the "T" post into the apartment and used it to beat the victim the death, hitting the ceiling with every up-swing strike.

Sure enough, the murder weapon was found discarded outside the apartment, and it was a five-foot metal fence post with a perfect "T" at the end. Phone records and phone ping locations showed that the suspect was at the scene at the time of the murder. The fence builder suspect was later arrested as he was found hiding out in the town of Cut and Shoot, Texas. The irony of the story is that the suspect did not choose to "cut" or "shoot" his victim, but his weapon of preference was the Texas "T" Post. Be like the inquisitive llama and question all things that make you go…Hmm.

# THE HONK OF THE MIGRATING GOOSE

*(Finding deception from the question)*

# CHAPTER 14

———◆———

Before I transferred into the Homicide Division, I spent years working the night-shift patrol in both good and bad neighborhoods. Our police department had a ride-along program where young recruits interested in law enforcement could ride with patrol officers to see if they really wanted to pursue policing as a career. I am happy to say that every ride-along recruit that ever rode with me ended up joining the police department at a later date. Some of them may be cursing me today, but I hope all are enjoying their chosen career. I often wonder if I missed my calling in recruiting because I was able to create a sense that a dangerous and dirty job could appear so fun and carefree.

As young recruits rode with me, I would explain to them that the job requires 90% communication with only 10% perspiration. In other words, you will do a lot more talking than fighting as a police officer. I always tried to introduce them to the different elements of cultures and different personalities of people, so they would know what to expect once in uniform. I would often take the recruits to a high crime area of town where street-level drug dealing was running rampant at all hours of the night. Certain streets in Houston are known for drugs as the dime store dealers migrate from corner to corner selling their illegal goods. I would explain to the recruit that as we turned onto the next street in the patrol car, there will be several shady looking characters standing on the street corner. Immediately, when they spot the patrol car, most of them will migrate back into the darkness but a few of them will stand there and pretend to be innocent.

I told one recruit that rode with me that we would approach the remaining alleged innocent bystanders and ask them what they were doing standing on a street corner in the middle of the night. I explained for the recruit to listen very carefully to the response that was given to us. He would soon be hearing the sound of a goose that knows that it should have migrated with the other geese. Sure enough, as I asked, "What are yall doing standing out here at three in the morning?" all of them answered together with a dumbfounded "Huuh?" As their response was given in perfect unison, it sounded more like geese sounding "Honk!" than someone actually inquiring about a question. Without me repeating the question to them, their lies started immediately rolling off their tongues with excuses like, "I thought the bus was still running," or "I'm waiting on my girl." I explained to the recruit that whenever you hear the sound of the "Honk!" like the migrating goose, then know that the next sentence spoken will be an untrue statement. I found this to be true in over two decades of law enforcement and it will be true two decades from now.

As you ask questions as a police investigator, some people will not like the question asked so they want to stall as they think of a lie. They stall in answering your question by asking their own question. Like the migrating geese honking away on the street corner rather than sharing the truth of drug sales to the police. The geese obviously heard the question, but stalled by saying, "Huuh?" before thinking of a deceptive statement to tell me. Whenever a suspect answers a question with question, then expect deception. Know that the goose is stalling before attempting to fly and migrate away with lies. The following questions show stalling answers to avoid the truth:

Q: "Did you kill Clyde?"

A: "Why would I kill him?"

Q: "Did you take the money?"

A: "Do you think I took it?"

Whenever a suspect asks for your opinion or thoughts, quickly bring him back to the truth that he needs to speak. You must control the interrogation and not let him interview you. Tell him, "My thoughts and feelings are irrelevant here; you know the truth so you need to speak the truth."

Q: "Were you at the bank?

A: "Who me?.. No"

Q: "Did you take the jewelry?"

A: "Did I take the jewelry?.. No."

Q: "What were you doing behind the house?"

A: "What house?"

Q: "Where is the gun?"

A: "Who said I had a gun?"

These types of interviews can be frustrating to police officers as we know that the suspect is stalling and avoiding the question. As you interview the proverbial goose, remain consistent and persistent to receive the truth. Never allow a suspect to know that you are getting tired or frustrated, or he will try to outlast you in the interview. Let him know your persistence by saying, "We could be here all day!" and that you will not let up or give up until he gets honest. You must outlast the lies so you can break through the hard-shell flesh to get to the soft soul. I interviewed a wife killer in a murder that had dumped his wife's body out on a ranch cow pasture. He continued to stall with his answers and asks me over a hundred questions as I asks him a hundred direct questions. I would ask him a question like:

Q: "What did she do to get you so angry?"

A: "Why does it matter now? My life is over."

I stayed and stuck with the direct questions and ignored his pondering statements to finally get a confession in the case. I left the interview room exhausted after almost 12 hours of questioning. His defense attorney attempted to discredit me during the trial as he stated in front of the jury "Well Sgt. Willson, I would have confessed too after 12 hours of being hounded and harassed by you." I simply told the attorney, "Counselor, you're right, you would have confessed if you murdered your wife and dumped her like trash in a field!" I painted a picture for the jury to see in their minds, so the defense attorney left me alone after that.

The proverbial goose will continue to "Honk" questions at you as questions are asked of him. Know that you are on the trail of truth, so stay with him and outlast his lies. Use statements like, "We need to explain how it happened," or "Tell your side of the story," to stop the frivolous questions. Keep him focused on the facts and let him know that you have empathy, but will endure longer than his questions. Stay in control of the interview and use the broth of truth to cook the goose.

# CRACKING THE COCONUT
# WITHOUT SPILLING THE MILK

*(Getting a clean confession)*

# CHAPTER 15

——◦◉◦——

"I killed him because he needed killing!" was the response given to me during a phone conversation as I started my first week in the Homicide Division. I learned that day that every time a high profile murder occurred in Houston and the media made it a lead story, Sweet Shirley would call the police to confess. She was a lonely and elderly black lady that craved attention, so would call the Homicide Division weekly to keep us updated on her concocted crime sprees. For years, whenever I answered phones at the front desk of the division, it seemed that 80-year-old Shirley was calling and confessing to the latest murder. She would tell me detailed stories of being the secret mistress of President Obama or giving birth to the love child of Michael Jackson. I would often transfer her call to the Sex Crimes Division, Juvenile Division, or Westside Division so all officers could enjoy her stories as much as I did. Westside Division would then transfer her to Northeast Division, but then they would often transfer her back to me to complete the never-ending cycle. As Shirley told the story and gave her confession, she would always end the statement with "That's pretty serious isn't it?" Shirley wanted attention, notoriety, and popularity so she tried to convince anyone who would listen that her story was serious.

As we interview suspects, we need to do just the opposite and portray the incident as "not serious." We need to make their involvement in the crime appear justified and reasonable and seem not-so-serious. In other words, minimizing the crime while minimizing their involvement, will maximize the discussion to talk about the crime. By allowing someone to downplay their responsibility and lessen their involvement to a certain crime, we are more likely to get a confession as they feel better talking about it.

A professional football player and star quarterback was being interviewed by sports reporters about secretly deflating footballs before the game started. It seemed that balls could be gripped better, thrown better, and caught better with less air pressure. Millions of dollars were at stake and millions of fans were upset because his team was playing in a championship game. However, the star quarterback downplayed the incident as he said, "This isn't ISIS, this isn't, you know, no one's dying!" He was trying to downplay the incident as he denied his involvement in deflating footballs. Sure enough, within a minute into the interview, the quarterback slipped up as they asked him if he was a cheater. He said, "I don't believe so" which does not sound very convincing because if he did not cheat, then why not just say so and emphatically tell us that he did not cheat. When someone says "I don't believe so", they are saying that based on their belief system, they don't think so but others would believe differently. As the quarterback was allowed to downplay the incident, he downplayed his involvement, so slipped up and gave us a sneak-peek into his soul.

As investigators holding the velvet-covered brick, we need to minimize the crime to make it appear less revolting and make it appear more socially acceptable. Sometimes, we have to put on our defense attorney thinking caps and create a defense for the suspect, so he will buy into the false theory and give us the truth. A good strategy is to suggest that an accident occurred and the outcome was different than desired by the suspect. Another strategy is to suggest that self-defense occurred, so the suspect was forced to make a decision that he would not normally make. However, we have to be very careful with these strategies as the suspect can cling to the theory and use it in his defense. We must make sure that physical evidence is there to dispute and discredit the false theory later in the interview, as the hard truth of the hard brick hits him. The following statements are examples that allow the suspect to minimize his actions and downplay his involvement in the crime:

A. "We're all humans, so we all make mistakes. Show people that you have a heart and tell your side of the story. You probably went into the wrong apartment and didn't know that was going to happen."

B. "Your wife was always nagging and dragging you down. You were just trying to do the right thing, but it was never good enough. We all reach our breaking points and snap, but you didn't intend to hurt her."

C. "You give your loyalty to your employer, but they don't appreciate your years of dedication. What you took was owed to you anyway. People will understand that you intended to pay it back in due time."

D. "Everybody knew he was a bully and had it coming to him. If you had not taken action, he was going to eventually hurt somebody. You had to protect yourself and do what was necessary."

E. "She walked in the club wearing that tight red dress. She knew that she was teasing and enticing you. We are men and we have needs, but people play games by provoking us."

I have used these statements to place blame on everyone but the suspect, so a false theory about the crime can be started and bought into. Often, the suspect will accept the theory and begin to use it in his defense as he tells his story. We must make sure that physical evidence is presented at the end of the interview, so the suspect is confronted with the actual truth and cannot cling to his distortions. These are simply ice breakers to get the guilty to talk.

One hardened gang member that I had interviewed bought into the self-defense story. He quickly started using my story to make it his own story, as he explained why he shot and killed a man in an apartment complex. The suspect had a hard shell exterior, but it cracked and the coconut milk flowed like a river as he spent twenty minutes telling me his slightly modified version of the story. I let him tell me great details about the shooting and killing of the man, before I threw the proverbial velvet-covered brick. I explained to him that the bullet strikes and all the witness statements confirmed that the victim was running away from him, not towards him. The suspect was told that the victim was unarmed and 33 feet away from him as he fired his gun repeatedly. I reminded him that he was the aggressor that ran down a flight of stairs and across a parking lot, as he caught up to kill the victim in supposed self-defense.

As the interview process is rolling along, you will draw more and more truth out of the suspect as you ask more questions. You will begin to notice a physical change in him as he lets his guard down and begins to trust you. His arms and legs will no longer be crossed and he will appear more emotionally open to you as he becomes more physically open to you. Often, the suspect will start to cry with real tears flowing as he lowers his head in shame. As the interviewer, you need to move your chair closer and closer to him as he draws closer to a confession. At this point, you must act as the soul searcher and help his soul bring forth the truth from his spirit. It is acceptable to gently touch his shoulder, arm, or hand and use your authority as a truth seeker to draw the truth from him. You are literally taking the truth that you know and connecting it to the truth that he knows to receive the confession of truth. Do not touch the suspect anywhere below the waist as this will send a sexual message, especially those involved with deviant sexual crimes. You are trying to send a spiritual message, so all contact should be made above the waist and close to the heart. At this point, you will be toe to toe and knee to knee with the suspect, but this is not a physical confrontation because you are drawing out a spiritual confession.

Some detectives have told me, "I am not really the touchy-feely type." However, you must fake it until you make it because this method will bring the greatest success in getting confessions. No contact means no impact. Jesus used this same strategy and was able to get demons to speak the truth and confess.

In the Bible at Luke 4:40 (TEV), "After sunset, all who had friends who were sick with various diseases brought them to Jesus. He placed his hands on every one of them and healed them all. Demons also went out from many people screaming, you are the son of God!" This is one of the few places in the Bible where even demons were speaking the truth to identify and announce Jesus. I am not saying that police officers should become exorcists of demons, but we should exercise the truth and make sure it is sought out in every case. We as police investigators want the guilty to confess to their crimes. We must help them as they identify with the truth, and they announce the truth in interviews. We must be willing to do what Jesus did as we study out his scriptures to do our jobs better. WWJD means What Would Jesus Do.

# PSYCHOS, WACKOS, &
WHICH WAY TO GO

*(Understanding the mind of a madman)*

# CHAPTER 16

———◆◆◆———

This next chapter is about the "Tale of Two Teds" in which two men with the same first name terrorized our country for many years with their hatred for humanity. Most everyone has heard of Ted Bundy, the serial killer; and Ted Kaczynski the serial bomber, so I wanted to use their lives to explain the mind of a psychopath and sociopath. There are thousands of pages of documents and thousands of hours of discussion debating the cause and effect of anti-personality disorders. Many criminologists and psychologists have debated the differences of a psychopath versus a sociopath as there are many gray areas. I certainly hold no degree in psychology and will not present myself as an expert in the field of study of the human mind. I am simply a policeman that has found a pattern and used it successfully as a basic principle. In law enforcement, we often analyze crimes and study criminals as there will always be certain patterns that exist to help us solve the crime. If we use our experience to conduct an experiment, then we will gain wisdom to know that the devil is in the details and what is needed to defeat him.

The first case study is Theodore (Ted) Robert Bundy born in Vermont in 1946. He was abandoned as a baby by his natural father, and his mother was reported as domineering and demanding of his success. Bundy grew up in a stable home and was drawn to academics early in his life, scoring 140 on an IQ test. He received an academic scholarship from Stanford University and earned a degree in psychology. He later enrolled as a law student at the University of Utah where he excelled once again. Bundy was charismatic, witty, good looking, and girls were attracted to him as he made friends easily. He went on a five-year killing campaign and is suspected of raping, torturing, and killing between 40 and 400 females from Washington to Florida. This coast to coast killer escaped from jail twice and would always cut and run as the police moved in closer to his crimes. He used multiple aliases and a fake ID to avoid capture and never settled anywhere very long. Bundy was able to blend in and socialize easily and could mix in with a crowd. Many of his victims trusted him before their death. He targeted college girls; his comfort zone and killing field was the college campus scene. Bundy had no sympathy of others but certainly understood sympathy, so he used it as a tool to trap his many victims. He would often put his arm in a fake sling or pretend to be handicapped, so unsuspecting female victims would feel sorry and offer to assist him. Upon his final arrest and after the trail of murders were uncovered, Bundy attempted to represent himself at his trial. He was executed in Florida in 1989. Bundy would be classified as a textbook Psychopath.

The next case study is Theodore (Ted) John Kaczynski, known as the Unabomber, born in Illinois in 1942. He was abandoned as a baby also, as he was quarantined in isolation for months at a hospital because of allergic reactions. During this time, he received no attention or affection from his parents as the hospital gave him treatment. Kaczynski was also drawn to academics and loved solving math problems; his IQ test was reported above 165. His home was stable and solid as his parents demanded excellence in academics from him as he studied the German, Spanish, and Latin language. He also received an academic scholarship and graduated from Harvard University before moving on as a Mathematics Professor at the University of California. Kaczynski was just the opposite of Bundy in social skills as he avoided human interaction. He never blended in or mixed in with any crowd and was always seen as a quiet outsider. Kaczynski had only one girlfriend in his entire life, but the relationship ended in bitterness as he wrote damaging words about her. After receiving complaints from his students about his shyness and unwillingness to interact, Professor Kaczynski left his job at the university to live a life of seclusion in the wilderness. He avoided making friends and avoided contact with family, even refusing to go to his own father's funeral.

He went on a 20-year campaign to send homemade bombs through the mail to college professors and airline executives. FBI investigators nick-named him the "Unabomber" because of his targeting of universities and airlines. However, he proudly wore the title because of being alone as "One bomber." Kaczynski built a small cabin on his isolated land in Lincoln, Montana, where he set up his laboratory for bomb making. He avoided detection from federal agents by sending his package bombs from random states far away from his home base. He would spend days riding a bicycle to the bus station, and then catch a bus to a major city in another state to mail his package bomb. After 20 years of torment and 16 bombs later, Kaczynski was turned in by his brother, after recognizing his writing style in a manifesto to the New York Times. He was arrested at his Montana cabin by multiple law enforcement officers; after he had just finished making another masterpiece of a bomb. I have visited his property in Lincoln, Montana, and it was obvious from threatening messages carved on trees around his land that he hated any outside intervention of people. Exactly as Bundy had done, Kaczynski represented himself in the courtroom, but agreed to life in prison rather than face the death penalty. Kaczynski would be classified as a textbook Sociopath.

Both these men had one motive in common, as they both had a mission to kill as many people as possible. They had a deep hatred for humanity because of perceived rejection by humanity. Both the psychopath and sociopath have no empathy, sympathy, or remorse for their crimes. They actually get gratification and entertainment from their illegal actions, receiving their pleasure through the pain of the victim. Their conscience has been burned and seared years ago, most likely from isolated or repeated cycles of childhood abandonment. Both the psychopath and sociopath will consider their fathers to have abandoned them or just weak in nature. Their mothers will be considered as domineering or demanding, so the combination of these two types of parenting characters can build a hidden rage like a ticking time bomb. The lack of attention from a father and the lack of affection from a mother can be a recipe for disaster. Thankfully, most people will not develop these psychotic tendencies, even with a bad childhood or checkered past. The major difference in the psychopath and the sociopath is that the psychopath can fake his feelings and mimic the compassion of others, as he has none of his own. The psychopath will use charisma and charm to mix, mingle, and manipulate others. The sociopath will avoid social interaction and work alone behind the scenes. The psychopath will attack from an open front and the sociopath will attack from a rear flank.

Both the psychopath and sociopath will be meticulous and leave few clues to their crimes. They are calm, calculated, and plan every detail so they can be difficult to catch. However, once captured, the psychopath and sociopath can be interviewed with success as you get into their world.

I received a double murder case where firefighters put out a house fire and discovered two bodies inside with their skulls crushed. The male victim was elderly and a long time respected pastor in the community. The female victim was his daughter visiting from California on vacation. A third victim, the pastor's elderly wife was a dementia patient with no memory of the incident. She was left unharmed in a back bedroom as the house was left burning. Thankfully, firefighters pulled her from the burning home just before smoke and flames overtook her. Surviving family members told me that a 20-year-old grandson lived in the house too, but he was nowhere to be found.

Good surveillance work by patrol officers checking around the victim's church brought the grandson into custody, as he pretended to go about his routine duties. He was brought into the Homicide Division and questioned about the incident. I had already researched his character through family members and knew that he showed symptoms of a sociopath. Within the first few minutes of the interview, he appeared shy and anti-social, so I knew that I needed to gain his trust to pull the truth from him. We began to talk about his childhood and feelings of being abandoned by his parents. He lived with his pastor grandfather, but everyone appeared too busy to give him any attention or affirmation. He told me that he played drums in the church band because he was too shy to be on center stage and sing the songs himself. He said that no one ever gave him a compliment on his musical skills and his parents did not care about him.

I connected with him emotionally by pulling up some of his music videos on the internet, and began to compliment him on his songs and talent. It seemed that he could easily entertain in front of a camera in the privacy of his bedroom, but he was out of his comfort zone in a social setting with people present. The Unabomber displayed the same characteristics and was very focused and talented in a private setting. He created his plan of attack, built bombs of mass destruction, and wrote his twenty thousand word manifesto all from the privacy and comfort of his cabin. A lesson learned here is that both of these sociopaths have their comfort zones, but will often clam up and shut down in a social environment.

As we looked at the 20-year-old suspect's music video filmed from his bedroom, I spotted a can of flammable spray in the background of the video. I realized that this was the same spray can found next to the bodies in the home used to start the fire. I asked him the direct question of "Is that the same spray can that you used to start the fire and burn the bodies?" He answered openly without hesitation that the can had a flammable spray in it, so he used it to chase his elderly grandfather down the hallway and burn him. He went on to explain that he burned both victims with the flammable spray as they fled from him to the kitchen and huddled together. He then crushed their skulls with a sledge hammer that he found in the garage, as both victims bled and burned helplessly on the floor.

The psychopath and sociopath have no real sympathy or regard for others, so it is very easy for them to talk about their crimes. They will often give great and graphic details of their crime without any remorse or hesitation. It is more about getting them to share a story about what happened to them, than sharing the story about what happened with the victim. In their mind, it is all about them so they have no compassion for other people and are totally engulfed in their own advancement. It is still a matter of getting past the flesh to get them to confess, and you must pull the soul towards the whole truth. However once there, hang on for the ride because you will be told every horrific detail. The horror from the victim and the gore of their action will be explained as they performed their psychotic rage.

# LLAMA LOADERS &
# PRACTICAL JOKERS

*(Canvassing the crime scene & beyond)*

# CHAPTER 17

When most people hear the word "canvas" they think of a piece of tightly stretched woven cloth used by artists to paint a masterpiece. When police investigators hear the word "canvass" they think of covering an area or community to find people that could be witnesses to a crime. However, both have a similar meaning in that before the artwork can start, the canvas must be stretched out as the picture is painted and created. The motive and meaning of a crime is better understood after a canvass has stretched out across the community, gathering all possible witnesses to paint a clear picture.

Being involved in law enforcement for so many years, I have made good friends with lots of good guys. When you risk your life with certain people, it becomes easier to share your life with those same people. One of my good friends lived near me in the country outside of Houston, so we rode together a few times as partners. I consider him a top-notch Patrol Sergeant and trust his judgment in handling confusing and clustered up crime scenes. He was a neighbor and good friend of mine so he understands my love for llamas, as he has helped me round up and load up a trailer full of them in the past. Both of us have the experience of being spit at and kicked at by angry non-compliant suspects and by angry non-compliant llamas as they hummed with inquisitive curiosity.

My sergeant friend called Homicide Division one night and informed me that he had arrived on Houston's craziest crime scene of the night. It seems that three male coworkers came in town on business and were staying at a motel for a few days. All three men were celebrating and drinking heavily as they arrived, so they visited several night clubs and topless bars around Houston. After a full night of partying, the three men went to their motel room to prepare for work the next morning. It was at this time, the men realized for the first time that their motel room only had two small beds, but they were three full sized men. They decided to flip a coin to see who would sleep together in the same bed and who would sleep peacefully alone. The coin was flipped and the winner declared his victory by beginning to tease the two losers and torment them about their close sleeping arrangements. The winner compared his two roommates to actors Steve Martin and John Candy, as they were also forced to cram together in a small motel bed in the movie <u>Planes & Trains.</u> The winner of the coin toss quickly became the ultimate loser, as he died after doing his standup comedy routine. His heart was punctured from a large fold-out buck knife as the two coworkers pretended to not know why.

My partner and I arrived on the homicide crime scene and began to interview the two remaining and surviving coworkers. My friend, the street-wise sergeant and llama wrangler, had already separated them in two different patrol cars before we arrived. The two told the exact same story and it appeared that they had rehearsed and perfected it before they decided to call 911. Some people call synchronized swimming a highly practiced sport, but I believe synchronized story telling can require just as much practice. They said that after the coin toss, the winner teased them before going into the bathroom to brush his teeth and prepare for bed. After several minutes, the victim returned to lay down on his bed. The coworkers said that the victim rolled into his bed, but he must have also rolled onto the blade of the buck knife as it stuck in his chest. Both coworkers called it a freak accident and appeared to be clueless to the crime. They both agreed that the folding buck knife belonged to the victim, suggesting that he must have left it in the bed and simply forgot about it as he laid on it.

As I studied the motel bed, I could see that all blood stains and spatter were on top of the blanket, sheets, and mattress cover, so the victim had been lying on top of the bed, but not in it. Another clue was that the blanket, the bed sheets, the fitted sheet, and the mattress cover all had an obvious knife slice through the material in the middle of the bed. The physical evidence showed us that a knife blade penetrated through the bed covering, so the precision-crafted knife was telling the truth but the witnesses were not. The knife was obviously under the covers but the victim was not. The crime scene screamed of things that make you go... hmm! The coworkers were interviewed further until they turned against each other and finally decided to get honest and get on the same side as the truth.

The truth of the story revealed that the victim did tease the two coworkers and hurt their feelings about sleeping together. He did go to the bathroom to brush his teeth as both men indicated. During the few minutes while the victim was gone and out of the room, the two coworkers decided to play a prank on him. They took his buck knife from the night stand and opened it up, exposing the six inch blade. They placed his knife under all the bed coverings and stuck the blade upward in the middle of the bed, penetrating the blanket, sheets, and mattress covering. As the victim came out of the bathroom, he yelled out "Sweet dreams, sissy boys!" as he performed a swan dive in the middle of his sabotaged bed. In the dimly lit motel room with his drunken motor skills, the victim did not notice the new shape of his neatly made bed. The bed covering now formed a perfect big top tent, holding the knife straight up to impale him and kill him in seconds.

I canvassed the entire motel premises searching for any witnesses that may have seen the three amigos fighting or partying before the incident. I knew that I needed an unbiased witness in the case to either confirm or contradict their story. The next day, I found the perfect witness that could explain how a knife could be held up so securely with just bed coverings. She was the motel maid and the lady that had made the bed with such precision and pride. She had worked at the motel for years and made over 100 beds a day. She made each bed in the same way using the same pattern each and every time. I followed her around for several hours as she showed me how to make a bed stretch tighter than a trampoline. I used one of the beds that she made as my test case and laboratory experiment. Sure enough, when the lady made a bed, it would easily support and secure a knife that could impale a person falling on it. The case was referred to the grand jury for possible manslaughter charges as premeditated murder was ruled out for the two pranksters.

Expert witnesses can be found in almost every case if you search hard enough and stretch the canvass far enough. True crime TV would suggest that the first 48 hours after a murder occurred is the most important time frame to solve the crime. However, I found it much more helpful to study the last 24 hours before the murder occurred and then the first 24 hours immediately after the murder. This method gives a clearer picture of what happened and a cleaner window of seeing the means, motive, and opportunity for the crime.

I once had a child-death case involving a horse, where an unruly stallion had stomped and crushed a four-year-old child that got under his feet. To be certain that the child's death was horse-related and not by human hands, I studied the behavior and activity of the horse 24 hours before the incident. Sometimes as we study unruly beasts and the bad behavior of people, we will see similar character flaws. I learned that the stallion was extremely aggressive and had attacked other horses as he roamed on acreage at his neighborhood stables. The horse was still very irritated and high-spirited, as the child attempted to ride him. I had no reliable or unbiased witnesses at the scene, so I used police officers from the Houston Mounted Patrol Division to study the case. Many of these saddle hardened officers had vast experiences and been injured themselves. They explained to me that Houston Mounted Patrol utilizes horses that are mares (females) or geldings (castrated males) and would never trust a high-spirited stallion around a child. They were able to create a scenario and explain how a spooked horse could go from flight animal to fight animal in a split second; crushing and killing a small child. I took one of the mounted patrol officers with me to spend time with the horse, and indeed the stallion became aggressive and attempted to charge and challenge us. It was the first time in my career that I considered using my Taser on a farm animal. As we look into the possibilities of how a crime occurred, we must be willing to knock on doors, walk the fields, or parade through horse manure. We must canvass the entire crime scene and canvass everything connected to the crime scene, so we can find witnesses to seal the deal, solve the crime, and seek the truth.

# EMPTY GRAVES & KARAOKE RAGE

*(Piecing the puzzle so it all makes sense)*

# CHAPTER 18

———◆◆———

I spoke with a well-versed atheist attorney once and he tried to explain away the Bible in one quick sentence. He told me that the Bible was just a collection of fairy tales of men running from floods, fires, plagues, pestilence, and the occasional evil villain. He believed that society was more likely to prove that Sasquatch rode a unicorn than the existence of a living God. I explained to him that oxygen and gravity were invisible too, but he could not take another breath or take another step without them. The intelligent atheist said that the Bible was full of contradictions and could not be considered a reliable source for living your life. I explained to him that the Bible is actually a book of decisions, and as we make decisions in our life then our decisions will make us. I told him for the sake of simplicity, we could divide the Bible into two parts. Two men (Adam and Jesus) both went to two trees (the tree in the garden and the Holy Cross) and both made two different decisions (one chose to sin and one chose to save).

We as an intelligent species must make a decision to either follow Adam or follow Jesus, as our entire future depends on that decision. Just as Adam brought sin into the world, every Adam since him has done the same thing. Jesus was the only man ever to walk the earth without sin, so he took our place and bled out at the cross to cover our sins. Any tainted and contaminated blood needs a blood transfusion for life to continue, so Jesus exchanged our sinful blood for his sinless blood. It took an old bloody wooden cross to get us across from this world into Heaven. If we are going to step from this physical life into a spiritual life, then we must make a decision about Jesus. He was either a lunatic that lied to us, or he is the Savior that died for us.

The atheist seemed intrigued by my answer, even though he was well versed and knew the Bible scriptures far better than me. His display of intelligence showed lots of head knowledge, but his heart was simply empty of any faith or hope. He still wanted to debate and present possible contradictions in the Bible. He said, "What about the gospels of Matthew, Mark, Luke, and John? They all told the same story about Jesus hanging, dying, and resurrecting, but didn't have their stories straight." I explained to the atheist that whenever a traumatic event takes place like a murder, then different witnesses will see things differently and from a different perspective. If everyone tells the same story in exactly the same way, then a good detective will know that the story was likely rehearsed and practiced, but actually considered trash and not the truth.

The place of supposed contradiction in the Bible can be found in four verses with four different witnesses reporting Jesus buried in the tomb. Matthew 28:2 (NKJV) states, "Behold, there was a great earthquake, for an angel of the Lord descended from heaven and came and rolled back the stone from the door, and sat on it." Mark 16:5(NKJV) states, "Entering the tomb, they saw a young man clothed in a long white robe sitting on the right side and they were alarmed." Luke 24:3-4(NKJV) states, "They went in and did not find the body of the Lord Jesus. They were greatly perplexed about this. Behold, two men stood by them in shining garments." John 20:12(NKJV) states, "She saw two angels in white sitting, one at the head and the other at the feet, where the body of Jesus had lain." Here is how your field notes should look at this point as you study the witness statements to this case:

* Matt says- 1 angel sitting outside
* Mark says- 1 man sitting inside
* Luke says- 2 men standing inside
* John says- 2 angels sitting inside

Those that try to discredit the Bible will use these four verses to show that a contradiction took place in the witness statements. Based on the witness testimony, can you determine if the witnesses are attempting to deceive us or did they all see the same thing from different perspective? The truth is that all four witnesses are telling the truth based on where they stood and what they saw at the tomb of Jesus.

Any police officer that has ever arrived on the scene of a critical incident understands the chaos of an active crime scene. When all hell breaks loose, it is hard to make sense or see clearly in the fog of war until the fog clears. As investigators, we must sort through the witness statements and pick out the pertinent facts that will help clear the fog to bring truth to the case. All four witnesses here mention angels or angelic looking men being present at the tomb. They either referred to them as angels or gave a physical description that would classify them as angels. If you never saw angels before in your entire life, you might also refer to them as "guys in shiny suits," or "dudes in bleached bath robes." Angels were reportedly seen outside the tomb and seen inside the tomb, so this tells us where the witnesses were located as they observed the event unfold. If you had just walked into a darkened tomb from a bright sunny day outside, then your eyes might take several seconds to adjust. During this time of dilated visual adjustment, one angel or even multiple angels could have stood up, sat down or even juggled bowling pins and you could have missed it. All four witness statements in the gospel were consistent and accurate to agree that angels were present and Jesus was no longer in the tomb. They later saw and spoke to Jesus, so it proved that he had conquered the grave. Their focus was on the Savior, so all the other images in the story were secondary. The moral of the story is that Jesus overcame the grave, and so will anyone who believes in him.

My partner and I received a Karaoke Club "Cantina" killing where a man was shot and murdered after he finished singing a karaoke song on stage. The shooter did not like the song selection or the tune of the singer, so he shot the victim in the head and simply fled the scene. Who would believe that singing off-key would cause the off-switch in your life to flip? The establishment was full of patrons and people were eating, drinking, and being merry just prior to gunfire ending the party.

As my partner and I arrived at the crime scene, we collected any possible witnesses that had knowledge of the incident. One of the witnesses was a cook in the kitchen and saw the event through the food pick-up window. She testified that a man appeared to be upset about something and had jumped up around the stage to confront the karaoke singer. She claimed to have heard multiple shots and then observed the victim lying dead on the floor. A second witness was in the club eating some Tex-Mex tacos and drinking beer at a booth with friends. She testified that she heard two gunshots across the room, and looked up to see a man shooting another man in the head. She saw the victim fall dead on the floor and then the shooter chased a woman out of the club with his gun. A third witness was in the parking lot and heard one gunshot coming from the club. She saw a man with a gun run out of the club and jump into a green car with another man and drive away. The shooter was followed by two females in a gray car. She looked in the club and also saw the victim lying dead on the floor.

Notice how all three witnesses gave bits and pieces of the murder as it unfolded from start to finish. From the cook in the kitchen to the parking lot patron, everyone had their piece of the story to tell. All three witnesses were different, so they saw the crime from a different angle and a different set of eyes. The witnesses saw the same shooter and same dead body, but from a different perspective. The three witnesses gave good details about some part of the murder even though some of their facts were lost in the fog of war. The facts of the case revealed that there were actually two gunshots fired in the club, so only one of the witnesses was right. Notice how witnesses are more likely to be wrong about what they hear than what they see. Another important fact was that the shooter was not chasing the woman out of the club as she was his girlfriend and leaving with him. The shooter jumped in a green car with his friend as two girls followed behind in a gray car, but no witnesses inside the club saw the escape occur. Each witness in the shooting gave bits and pieces of accurate facts to create the picture of what happened during the shooting. The case was cleared and an arrest was made by our Homicide Chicano Squad as they shook the bushes and located the shooter. All the witnesses were instrumental as well; they played their part in putting the puzzle together.

As investigators, we should not discount or discredit a witness simply because they do not appear to have all their facts straight. A well respected Harris County District Attorney once said, "Sometimes you got to go to Hell to find your witnesses, so use them and don't abuse them." If all someone knows about an incident is that a green car sped away or two men in shiny garments were standing there, then you have received one more piece to your puzzle.

# WHISTLING PAST THE CEMETERY

*(Seeking justice through the injustice)*

# CHAPTER 19

———=◦(◉)◦=———

Law enforcement is one of the most unique careers that a person could pursue. Nowhere else can you be bored out your mind one minute, and then be fighting for your life the next minute. You will go from total disappointment to divine appointment in a split second to save a life, and adrenalin is your energy drink. Police officers are expected to go from 0 to 100 in one second, but the media can take us back from heroes to zeroes in a second as well. Nowhere else can you be praised by your peers one day, and yet be persecuted by the press the next day for the same incident. Policing is where you are expected to be tough and tender at the same time, and yet leave your opinions and feelings at home. I believe that God has ordained inside the heart of every police officer the desire to pursue the objective with everything you have, and accomplish the mission with everything you are. I have witnessed courageous officers take their last breath on the "thin blue line," and attended numerous funerals of friends that gave all that they had.

Jesus said it best in John 15:13 (TEV), "The greatest love you can have for your friends is to give your life for them." It is an amazing and rewarding career in law enforcement where we fight for the weak and speak up for the meek.

Policing has the only work place occupation where we can make jokes about the caliber of weapon that we carry, and people will actually laugh. I was asked once about an old revolver pistol that I had on my hip, "Is that a .357 in your holster?" I quickly answered, "It's a .357 or .358, whatever it takes to do the job!" Later on, I had purchased a more modern weapon and was asked, "Why do you carry a .45 automatic?" I quickly answered again, "Because they don't make a .46 automatic yet!" I have always said that policing is one of the few jobs where you will want to wash your hands before and after you go to the restroom. Occasionally, people have asked me what it was like being a big city Homicide Detective. I often explain it by saying, "It's like living in a world of chaos that is occasionally interrupted by order." I have written thousands of pages of police reports and came to one simple conclusion. In the fog of war and the center of the chaos, there are only two groups of people; "Those fighting to save life and those fighting to take life."

Every police officer starts their career fresh with great expectations of how things should go and how things should unfold. However, after a few years in the uniform, we realize that things will only unfold perfectly in an imaginary perfect world and we don't patrol in that fantasy place. We become survivalist as we see so much death and destruction, so we begin collecting a supply of survival tools. We attempt to obtain better weapons and better lighting, so better battle gear becomes our battle cry. We come to understand that "Justin Case" is not a person, but a lifestyle of how we live with just-in-case. As we grow into veteran officers, we realize that there is safety in numbers and we are a police force, and not just police individuals. We are well-trained and well-equipped, so have the wisdom of the great sheep dog to know that the ravenous pack of wolves seek out the weak, lame, and lone sheep. Over time and after many battle scars, the veteran officer comes to understand that his greatest survival weapon is his mind. The Bible explains our thought process in Proverbs 23:7 (NKJV) "As he thinks in heart, so is he." In other words, if you think you have lost the cause or think you have won the cause, either way you are right.

If we just "whistle past the cemetery" and ignore the cries and calls of those needing our help seeking justice; we ourselves will become helpless over time. If we limit our own abilities to accomplish our assignment as we become jaded and negative in life, then we will become ineffective as officers. God wants us to have faith and not fear as we perform our duties, as faith is a motivator and fear is a paralyzer. Faith and fear can be defined by the same definition, but with completely different meanings. Both are the belief system that something will occur before we have actually seen it occur. Fear is believing that something bad will happen. Faith is believing that something good will happen. As police officers, we must stay positive and have hope even when all the world appears hopeless. This is what allows a wounded officer to keep shooting and an injured officer to keep fighting, because victory belongs to those that don't quit. Apostle Paul said it best in the Bible at 2 Timothy 4:7 (TEV), "I have fought the good fight, I have finished the race, I have kept the faith."

In August of 1990, I was a young energetic patrol officer working the night shift, seldom taking a vacation day or sick day. In my mind, law enforcement could not be enforced without me, so I showed up early and stayed late for work. A call went out one night about a suspicious vehicle being abandoned near a wooded area in West Houston. The car had been reported missing the day before by concerned parents, and a young pretty female was the missing driver. As officers searched the wooded area around the car, the female's body was discovered deep in the woods lying face down in the brush. She had been stripped of her clothing, tied up, and violently raped before being slashed and mutilated with a very sharp blade. As I looked at the body of the victim, I could see that whoever committed this barbaric act to this beautiful girl truly hated humanity, as this was an up-close and personal killing.

The female was last seen with her boyfriend at a local dance club the previous night, but he could not be located. Naturally, the boyfriend was considered a person of interest as police investigators attempted to find him. I was given the boring solo assignment of staying at the crime scene all night and detaining the boyfriend, when or if he returned to the woods. I remember sitting alone in my patrol car with one hand on my pistol and the other hand on my police radio, watching and waiting for the darkness to produce the killer. I began to let fear creep into my mind and imagined that the killer must be eight feet tall and bullet proof, so I sat paralyzed in my patrol car. The mind is a powerful weapon either for us or against us, and I had allowed my patrol car to become my sanctuary to keep evil far away. After many hours of sitting idle, my legs began to go to sleep, although I was wide awake and needed to pee in the worst way. I began to talk with God about my situation and suddenly remembered that God talked all about fear in the Bible. In fact, God tells us to "Fear not" 365 times throughout the Bible; he knows that we will encounter it 365 days a year.

As I sat alone in the darkness, I remembered that I had taken an oath as a police officer to seek justice and not run from it. At this point, I had to make a decision if I would be a man or a mouse and if I would stand on faith or sit in fear. Suddenly, I felt the courage of the shepherd boy David as he killed the giant Goliath. I jumped from the patrol car quoting David and declaring, "Who is this uncircumcised killer that would challenge my faith?" I realized that I could sit all night and wait for investigators to search for witnesses and work the case, or I could begin my own search of the woods. Of course, there was the motivation of needing to pee that lingered in my mind too. As I started the one-man grid pattern search of the woods, the starting point would be from where the female was found and slowly working outward. I walked several hundred yards through the thick vegetation and found the perfect hollow tree that would be a make-shift urinal. As I unzipped my uniform pants and enjoyed nature while making a nature call, I suddenly felt an uneasy feeling that I was being watched.

I looked through the dark wooded area and as my eyes adjusted, I saw a young male staring at me as he sat Indian style under a distant tree. I left my zipper down as I pulled my pistol out and pointed it at him demanding "GET ON THE GROUND!" The male just stared and ignored my commands, so I carefully moved in closer for a better shot. As I moved towards the young male under the tree, I realized that he was tied to the tree and being restrained in several places. As I moved in even closer, still pointing a flash light and pistol at him, I realized that he was the boyfriend of the female victim. His throat had been sliced open almost to the point of decapitation and he was obviously dead. I had waited all night for the deadly beast to appear, and suddenly the dead boyfriend appeared. My theory, thoughts, and everything that I imagined about the boyfriend was totally wrong. The Zipper-Head is not the one that makes mistakes, the Zipper-Head is the one that doesn't learn from his mistakes. Lessons can be learned even with your zipper down.

As of 2014, "The Lovers' Lane" killing remained unsolved as one of Houston's most notorious cold case murders. The young couple was killed by an unknown assailant as he tied them up before butchering them in the isolated woods. I learned a valuable lesson from this case as I prepared and trained to become a Homicide Detective. It has helped me in many murder cases since as I always keep an open mind and no longer jump to quick conclusions. Another lesson learned was to stand on faith and allow it be a motivator, and never sit in fear or allow it to be a paralyzer. We must become fearless in life, rather than hopeless looking at death.

# GOOD GUYS, BAD GUYS, & FORGIVEN GUYS

*(Who we are & who we become)*

# CHAPTER 20

In law enforcement, each one of us has a different assignment and different jurisdiction to cover. Whether you work for a federal agency, state agency, county agency, or city agency, you still have your marching orders and objectives to achieve. All the branches of law enforcement were put in place for the common cause of keeping evildoers from overthrowing justice and order. The FBI Agent, Secret Service Agent, State Trooper, Deputy Sheriff, Deputy Constable, and Municipal Police Officer all have their boundaries of the battlefield in which they fight, and the common enemy is called "Evil."

For the most part, law enforcement is admired and respected in society as the barrier and buffer between that which is good, and that which is evil. We are doing a good job for a good cause with good character, so naturally think of ourselves as good people. However, this mindset can put us in a very dangerous place as we accomplish much in our physical lives, but become complacent in our spiritual lives. There are two sides to every coin. It is equivalent to the officer that cautiously watched the right hand of the left-handed suspect, so he missed the movement of the weapon that was pointed at him. We can be diligent, obedient, and dedicated, and still miss out on seeing the big picture of what is occurring. Being a good guy does not give us a ticket to Heaven, but being a forgiven guy does.

We must ask God for forgiveness as he gives us fresh starts and new beginnings. The Bible is crystal clear in Romans 3:23 (HCSB), "For all have sinned and fallen short of the glory of God." Every person that has ever walked this Earth has sinned and broken God's law, except for Jesus. I would be considered a good athlete if I could throw the perfect fast ball with perfect precision to strike out every batter that steps up to the plate. However, if I throw a ball trying to reach Heaven, I will "fall short" as the Bible says and miserably miss my target. Our accomplishments on Earth fall short of anything in Heaven, so our worldly achievements will not get us to Heaven. God is not impressed with what we can do because he wants us to focus on what he already did. Two thousand years ago, He sent his son Jesus to give us a blood transfusion to exchange our sinful blood for his sinless blood.

Some may say "Well, I'm not a bad guy because I haven't murdered anybody so compared to others, my rap sheet looks ok." God will not acquit us or excuse us on the actions of others, as it is our own actions under indictment. The devil will be the accuser of us all according to Revelation

12:10 (NKJV). The Bible is very clear that if we break one of the Ten Commandments, then we have broken all of the Ten Commandments. There are no felonies or misdemeanors in God's courtroom; all crimes are considered a capital punishment death sentence. A perfect judge must administer perfect justice, because God loves us but also loves justice. Envy is in the same category as extortion and lust is in the same category as money laundering. Murder and slander carry the same degree of punishment in God's General Orders. God says it in James 2:10 (HCSB), "For whoever keeps the entire law, and yet fails at one point, is guilty of breaking it all."

As we read God's Code of Criminal Procedures of violating the law, it appears like God's law makes it impossible to get to Heaven. After all, every one of us has violated the law in some capacity; God has raised the bar too high for us to reach. However, God never intended for us to get to Heaven by following his law, he intended for us to get to Heaven by following his love. John 3:16 (NKJV) states, "For God so loved the world that he gave his only begotten Son, that whoever believes in him should not perish but have eternal life." We are not saved by doing good works, we are saved for doing good works. Once we are saved, then God gives us the ultimate assignment of saving others. The beauty of the story is found in Romans 5:8 (NKJV), "While we were still sinners, Christ died for us." We do not have to be perfect people, just perfectly forgiven people.

The Bible says in Hebrews 11:6 (HCSB), "Now without faith, it is impossible to please God. For the one who draws near to Him must believe that He exists and rewards those who seek Him." The character of a Christian should exhibit peace, patience, kindness, goodness, and self-control because the heart of a Christian knows that his future is secure.

I have heard some people say that Hell is a state of mind or Hell is right here on Earth. Some people even try to down play their death by saying "I'll be pushing up daisies" or "I'll be a box lunch for worms" to explain the afterlife for them. Hundreds of years ago, paranoid pirates sailing the open seas on rickety ships told each other, "I'll be in Davy Jones' locker." However, the Bible tells us in Hebrews 9:27 (NKJV), "It is appointed for men to die once, but after this the judgment." There is no locker, lounge, or lodge available to us, but simply a courtroom as we pass from this life into the next. The devil would prefer to have us think that Hell is not a real place because misery loves company, so he wants us with him. The Bible states over 50 times throughout the scriptures that Hell is a physical place of fire, torment, and torture. Revelation 21:8 (NKJV) states, "The cowardly, unbelieving, abominable, murderers, sexually immoral, sorcerers, idolaters, and all liars shall have their part in the lake which burns with fire and brimstone, which is the second death." God does not send people to Hell because he has rejected them; people go to Hell because they have rejected God. Our salvation through Christ is a free gift for all to receive, but some people refuse to open the gift so never receive it. We all hold the winning lottery ticket of life, but some people never cash it in.

My prayer is that every law enforcement officer would come to the place of trusting Jesus with their eternal life. My hope is that the band of brothers never loses one as an abandoned brother. We step into dangerous situations in our physical lives, as we trust ballistic shields and bullet proof vests to save us. We need to walk with that same assurance in our spiritual lives as we trust Jesus to save us. God never says that we should be more religious, but he does desire to have a deeper relationship with us. God is our Creator and we are his creation, so he loves us and wants to spend time with us. We have our part to do as Christians and God will always do his part. 1 Thessalonians 5:23 (TEV) states, "May the God who gives us peace make you holy in every way and keep your whole being - spirit, soul, and body - free from every fault at the coming of our Lord Jesus Christ."

It is no accident that you are reading this book and made it to the last chapter and the last paragraph. This book was written about getting confessions from the guilty, but God is seeking a confession from all of us. The way to salvation and eternal life in Heaven is admitting that we are sinners, and we desperately need a Savior. We will never seek a cure for a disease, if we do not believe the disease exist. Romans 10:9 (HCSB) says, "If you confess with your mouth, Jesus is Lord, and believe in your heart that God raised Him from the dead, you will be saved." As we grow in our relationship with God, we need to relate with him and talk with him daily just like a friend. The Bible says in 1 Thessalonians 5:17-18 (TEV) to, "Pray at all times, be thankful in all circumstances. This is what God wants from you in your life in union with Christ Jesus." As we take our assignment in life, we need to take God at his promise in our life; that he will provide cover and concealment through the fire-fight. God will never leave us or forsake us as a partner, and he will provide the helmet of salvation and shield of faith in battle. Even as we take our last breath, God will make sure that our name is called at the final roll call.

# THE POLICE
# OFFICERS PRAYER

"Father God in Heaven, forgive me of my sin and when I fall short of my mission. Lord Jesus, I know that you love me because you died for me, so today let me live for you. Holy Spirit, guide me and give me clear decision making, everywhere I place my heart and hands. Lord, as your word says; "Let no weapon formed against me prosper," as I walk through any alley or valley of darkness. Let my aim and my actions be accurate and my motives be true to you in everything I do. In Jesus name I pray these things, Amen."

# ABOUT THE AUTHOR

Retired Homicide Sergeant JJ.Willson, spends his time these days pulling Rainbow Trout out of the "Mighty Mo" River in Montana. With his badge and gun on a shelf; life now consists of chopping firewood, fixing fences, and trying to decide which wine goes best with trout. The only killers in his life now are the rogue bears and mountain lions that attempt to make a meal out of his pet llama named Captain Jack. He lives happily ever after with his life-long wife, three loving children, and multiplying grandchildren. His strategy for living is the same one that Jesus had as he walked the Earth. Live, laugh, love, and leave this world better than you found it.

# REFERENCES

All scriptures and biblical research of FINDING TRUTH came from THE HOLY BIBLE. Any scripture that is labeled with the source and in quotation will indicate the source of publication. Permission was granted from the following publishers:

* Scripture taken from the New King James Version (NKJV): Copyright 1982 by Thomas Nelson Inc. Used by permission. All rights reserved.
* Scripture taken from Todays English Version (TEV): Second Edition, Copyright 1992 Old Testament: American Bible Society 1976, 1992 New Testament: American Bible Society 1966, 1971, 1976, 1992.
* Scripture quotations marked (HCSB) have been taken from the Holman Christian Standard Bible. Copyright 1999, 2000, 2002, 2003, 2009 by Holman Bible Publishers. Used by permission. Holman Christian Standard Bible, Holman CSB, and HCSB are federally registered trademarks of Holman Bible Publishers.